CHARTING INTELLECTUAL DEVELOPMENT

CHARTING
INTELLECTUAL
DEVELOPMENT

A PRACTICAL GUIDE TO PIAGETIAN TASKS

By

RUTH FORMANEK, Ph.D.

Professor of Elementary Education
Hofstra University
Clinical Psychologist
Jewish Community Services

and

ANITA GURIAN, M.Ed.

School Psychologist
Learning Disabilities Specialist

Illustrations by
David Formanek

CHARLES C THOMAS • PUBLISHER
Springfield • Illinois • U.S.A.

Published and Distributed Throughout the World by

CHARLES C THOMAS • PUBLISHER

Bannerstone House

301-327 East Lawrence Avenue, Springfield, Illinois, U.S.A.

© *1976, by* CHARLES C THOMAS • PUBLISHER

ISBN 0-398-03449-4 (cloth)
ISBN 0-398-03450-8 (paper)

Library of Congress Catalog Card Number: 75-8919

*With THOMAS BOOKS careful attention is given to all details of
manufacturing and design. It is the Publisher's desire to present books that are
satisfactory as to their physical qualities and artistic possibilities and
appropriate for their particular use. THOMAS BOOKS will be true to those
laws of quality that assure a good name and good will.*

Printed in the United States of America
R-1

Library of Congress Cataloging in Publication Data

Formanek, Ruth.
    Charting intellectual development.

    Bibliography: p.
    1. Cognition (Child psychology) 2. Piaget, Jean,
1896–   I. Gurian, Anita, joint author.
II. Title.
BF723.C5F67   155.4'13   75-8919
ISBN 0-398-03449-4
ISBN 0-398-03450-8 pbk.

PREFACE

This guide is dedicated to Jean Piaget, Bärbel Inhelder, and their co-workers, whose theories about cognitive development have had a major impact on all those concerned with children. They have enriched our understanding and we express our gratitude.

While we have based our text on their work, we take responsibility for its simplification and occasional reinterpretation.

We owe a particular debt to the children whose responses gave us a new appreciation of their imaginative and inventive thinking.

Family, friends, students, and colleagues have aided us at various stages and in innumerable ways. In particular, we want to thank Selma Greenberg, Bernard Gurian, Barbara Kimmel Diamond, Marilyn Maxwell, Greta Morine, Mary Ann Pulaski, Leonard Rack, and Raymond Scheele.

R.F.
A.G.

v

CONTENTS

CHARTING INTELLECTUAL DEVELOPMENT

Chapter 1

INTRODUCTION

Adults as well as children can learn better by doing things than by being told about them.

Jean Piaget

TRADITIONAL notions of how children think, communicate, learn, and develop are being re-examined by educators, clinicians, social scientists, and others working with children, in the light of the work of Jean Piaget. In the course of his research, Piaget devised methods of conducting interviews and experiments with children. The purpose of these interviews and experiments, the tasks, is to reveal the children's thinking strategies at different stages of cognitive, or intellectual development. This book, planned in response to students' difficulties with the predominantly theoretical emphasis of books about Piaget, is a practical, action-oriented guide to Piagetian tasks. Performing Piaget's tasks with children of varying ages, as described in this guide, will enhance one's ability to observe and to chart the acquisition and evolution of the stages of cognitive growth. Learning to question children in a one-to-one situation sharpens the skills of observing and listening, skills that yield valuable insights into the intellectual difficulties children encounter in the solution of problems. Speaking, observing, and listening to children, one is alerted to the gaps between child and adult thought processes. In referring to researchers working with children, Piaget has said, ". . . they see how difficult it is to make themselves understood by children, and to understand what children are saying."

Those readers primarily interested in children's cognitive development may use the tasks which follow to collect data for case studies or for research purposes. Teachers will find the tasks useful not only for providing information about the levels of children's thinking, but also in making decisions on curriculum content and the modes of teaching appropriate to different ages. For example, the teacher might be interested in whether or not a child conserves, since the teaching of subject matter such as liquid measurement depends on such knowledge. Younger children may be confused by the writing of numbers: for example, do written numbers mean the same thing no matter how they are written? Might not a large **8** contain more than a small **8** ? The importance of concepts of classification to the teaching of subjects such as reading and biology is equally obvious. Similarly, the clinician may find the development of concepts about dreams, family relationships, or life of interest in psychodiagnostic testing or in the therapeutic situation.

While this guide does not aim at exhaustive coverage of Piagetian ideas, it consists of a selected but representative number of tasks dealing with the acquisition of such major ideas or concepts as conservation, classification, cause-and-effect relationships, time, space, etc. including brief introductions to each section. The introductions consist of whatever theoretical notions are essential to the understanding of the acquisition and development of the concepts tested by the tasks.

We are fully aware that we do not do justice to Piaget's rich and complex theories. We have included only those theoretical notions we considered necessary to the first working encounter with children's cognitive development. It is to be hoped that the reader's own explorations of children's ideas by means of our instructions will furnish him with a first concrete experience to serve as a springboard for further theoretical study. For this purpose, we are suggesting a list of relevant books and films.

For inclusion in this guide, we have chosen those tasks which require simple materials, yet yield meaningful results. In all cases, we have used a standardized format, simplified the tasks, and explained Piagetian terms. In several cases, the content of the tasks has been adapted to suit American conditions.

DEMONSTRATION TASK

To give an example of our format, let us consider a task which demonstrates a basic Piagetian notion, the concept of *conservation*. Piaget defines conservation as the idea that some properties of a substance, such as amount or weight, remain the same, are invariant, are *conserved*, despite certain transformations. A substance may be transformed, or undergo a change, such as in shape, which alters its appearance, and yet the substance retains both its original amount and its weight. The child acquires the concept of conservation gradually, and Piaget's methods enable us to observe its acquisition and development. The following format will be used throughout this guide.

* * *

Question: **Does the child understand the concept of** *conservation of substance?*

Materials: Clay

Instructions:
(Place two equal balls of clay in front of the child.)

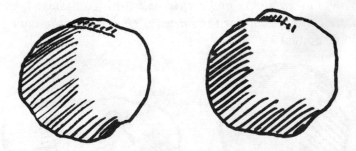

E:* Do both balls have the same amount of clay?
(Note how the child determines equality. Does he measure in some way? Let him adjust amounts if he so desires. The child must agree that the amounts are equal before proceeding.)

Transformation A

E: Now I'm going to flatten this ball into a pancake (do so). Which has more clay, the ball or the pancake? Or do they both have the same amount?
(Child responds. He need not agree that the amounts are equal.)

---

*E Signifies experimenter.

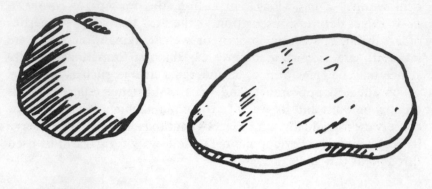

E: *Why did you say that* . . . . . ?
(Child responds. Experimenter returns the clay to its original state, that is, two balls of equal size).

Transformation B

E: *Now I'm going to make this ball into a sausage. Which has more clay, the ball, or the sausage? Or are they the same?*
(Child responds)

E: *Why did you say* . . . . . ?
(Return the clay to its original state.)

Transformation C

E: *Now I'm going to break one ball up into little pieces. Which has more clay, the ball, or the pieces? Or are they the same?*
(Child responds)

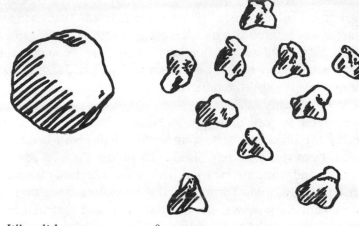

E: Why did you say . . . . . ?

Analysis

What do we learn from the results of this experiment? The child *under five years of age** usually has not acquired the concept of conservation of substance and generally makes judgments based on only one aspect or dimension of the clay; that is, he may consider its length, its width, or its height. In any case, he is unable to deal with more than one factor at a time. In addition to his inability to deal with two factors simultaneously, the child does not yet know that the clay sausage can be rolled back again into a ball, or reversed. He does not know that the *amount* of clay remains the same, that only its *shape* has changed. The child under five will often state that the ball has more clay because it is thicker, or wider, or that the sausage has more clay because it's longer, etc.

The child of *six to seven years old* is usually in a transitional stage in regard to this concept. He is uncertain whether the amounts are the same or not, because he has not as yet generalized the logical principle that a substance may undergo a change in appearance and still remain the same quantity. He will often say, "I don't know; it looks like this one has more," or "You really didn't put more in it, but I guess it's more."

---

*All ages are approximate. Piaget's goal is to study the development of thinking, not to furnish age norms.

The child of *eight years or older* has usually acquired the notion of conservation of substance. He consistently sees that changes in length are compensated for by changes in width. He will typically say, "You didn't add any or take any away," or "You can roll it back into a ball, and it will be the same," or "It doesn't matter what shape it is, it's still the same amount."

If you prefer to read more about Piaget's ideas before actually performing the tasks, the following section will prove helpful. At this point, however, you may choose to follow Piaget's advice to "do things" and continue with other tasks. The tasks have been organized into the same format as the preceding one, that is, a brief statement of purpose, list of materials, and instructions. A guide to the analysis of the children's responses follows each task, including sample responses meant to serve as references with which to match obtained responses. The tasks cover a wide range of concepts and need not be administered in order. Selection of the tasks should be governed by the experimenter's interest as well as by the age of the subject.

ORIENTATION

Can we assume that there is a difference between the thought of adults and the thought of children? Are thinking children merely miniature thinking adults? Do children and adults differ only in extent of experience or in strategies of acquisition of knowledge? Or in proficiency of language usage? Are adults more adequate thinkers because they have lived longer, acquired more information, and can express themselves with the aid of richer vocabularies? Are physical and emotional maturation correlated to intellectual maturation? Piaget and other researchers have suggested that children not only lack experience, information, and extensive vocabularies, but that the quality of their thinking is vastly different from that of adults. The child's thought should be viewed as part of a lengthy and complex organizing process which begins with an inability to comprehend one's surroundings. This first infantile stage is followed by misconceptions and fragments of ideas, slowly leading to intuitive and partial comprehension, and finally to adequate approximations of reality. While we laugh and marvel at children's creativity, we should remember that they are trying to make sense of their environment, that they are independent, inventive thinkers.

Periods of Cognitive Development

The environment furnishes the same information to adults and children alike, yet the manner in which the information is utilized differs. The processing of the information, i.e. the manner in which we interact with and discover our environment, is necessarily different at different periods of cognitive growth. The growing child, interacting with his environment, constructs for himself a picture of the environment; that is, he builds up mental representations of his world. The type of representation he builds up differs depending on his age and his picture of the world becomes increasingly more complex and more realistic as he gets older.

Piaget classifies cognitive development into four periods which refer to types of thinking. The periods are somewhat related to age; however, a child does not automatically reach a given period as he reaches a given age. Rather, the child's entry into a new period of cognitive development depends upon his capacity to process information in certain ways. The periods occur in invariant order; one can neither skip periods nor change their sequence. The following is a brief sketch of Piaget's periods of cognitive development.

Sensory-motor period

Piaget calls the first period, lasting from birth to about two years of age, the sensory-motor period. Within the first few months of life, the newborn's reflexes, such as sucking, grasping, etc. are modified, adapted, and elaborated on the basis of interactions with things and with people. For example, the motion of sucking, present at birth, adapts to the shape of nipples, of bottle or breast, or to the thumb. Slightly modified sucking movements are also used when a spoon with solid food is introduced. By means of these adaptations, the infant acquires a practical knowledge about bottle, breast, thumb, spoon, etc. After several months of modifying, adapting, and elaborating reflexes, the infant becomes capable of coordinating two reflexes. For example, he can now see what he grasps and can grasp what he sees. He has coordinated grasping and vision and can more effectively cope with the information available to him. As he grows older, he begins to imitate actions, to anticipate events, and to show the beginnings of curiosity. Toward the end of the first year of life, a child has already acquired, in elementary form, a number of important ideas about his world. He has learned, among other things, that certain events appear in sequence; he is fed after intervals of crying and waiting (concept of time), his crying seems to cause someone to feed him (cause-and-effect relationships); an object, when released from his grasp, will fall (concepts of space and gravity). Until seven months of age an infant believes that an object which has disappeared from view has ceased to exist and he will not search for it; that is, the infant has not yet acquired the notion of *the permanence of objects.* These are examples of early and elementary concepts but deal with important aspects of the world and are essential to an understanding of the world and of one's place in it.

Before the child is two years old, he has begun to use language and is capable of the elementary use of other symbols. For example, he now recognizes pictures of familiar objects, plays simple games, etc.

Preoperational Period — Two to Seven Years *

1. Preconceptual subperiod: 2 to 4 years.
2. Intuitive subperiod: 4 to 7 years.

New and improved strategies for information processing are constantly evolving. While the very young child can perform simple actions which give him practical knowledge, he lacks proficiency of language. Acquisition of language gives the growing child a powerful additional technique in his exploration of his

---

*"Operation" will be defined on page 14.

environment. The four-year-old, for example, is now able to augment previously acquired practical knowledge by asking questions about what makes a toy fall when he releases it, or why night comes after dinner. He has not forgotten previous knowledge gained from action; he integrates it into his storehouse of experiences, adds to it and modifies it by means of new and more adequate strategies. Each period is thus a prerequisite for the following one.

During the intuitive subperiod, the four to seven-year-old child continues to acquire information unsystematically from various sources. Although he seems to understand concepts intuitively, he lacks strategies of acquiring knowledge systematically. The game "Twenty Questions" is an example of a systematic strategy to gain information and is rarely played by young children. The thinking of the child in the intuitive subperiod is marked by inconsistencies and lack of logical organization. At times he responds to questioning logically and consistently, and then suddenly changes course and fails to follow through an apparently simple sequence of reasoning.

The casual, piecemeal acquisition of frequently conflicting bits of information over a period of several years precedes the formation of a stable, consistent and logical conceptual framework at the age of about eight years. Moreover, the child in the intuitive subperiod is egocentric; that is, he is unable to understand how the world looks from a point of view other than his own. His limited and unsystematic acquisition of information and his egocentrism tend to keep his focus limited and blurred, and his judgments tend to be based on the appearance of things only. Children at this age are gullible, ready to believe in tall tales and magic.

Another limitation to his acquisition of concepts is the child's inability to deal with more than one variable at a time. He finds it difficult to consider more than one aspect of the same situation. For example, in the conservation experiment described in the previous section, the child may actually have observed the experimenter make the transformation, e.g. change the shape of the clay. He nevertheless may respond solely to the appearance of the clay, to one of its obvious dimensions: perhaps width alone, perhaps length alone. It is unlikely that he will understand the compensation of width for length, or vice versa. He judges by what he sees at the moment without regard to what was or what will be. He may state that now there is more clay or less clay despite the fact that he has seen the ball transformed into a sausage. Judgments of the child in the intuitive subperiod are frequently inconsistent since they lack underlying logical principles. For example, the principle necessary to judge the changed appearance of the clay states that the quantity of a substance remains the same despite changes in its appearance, provided nothing is added or taken away.

Concrete Operational Period — Seven to Eleven Years

The child in the period of concrete operations is less egocentric and is capable of dealing with two variables at the same time. The appearance of things exerts less influence on judgments such as those called for in the case of the conservation experiment previously described. In that experiment the child between the ages of seven and eleven may note that the shape of the substance changed, but he is no longer unduly influenced by its changed appearance. Rather, he responds on the basis of the principle, which dictates that the substance must have remained the same since nothing was added or taken away.

Judgments of the child at this stage tend to be stable and consistent. In general, however, the thinking of the child in the concrete operational period, while more logical and efficient than his thinking at earlier periods, is still tied to the presence of concrete materials. The child is not as yet a proficient, abstract thinker. Although he has made a beginning, he cannot hypothesize well or deal exhaustively with all the possibilities inherent in the solution of a problem.

Formal Operational Period — Eleven Years On

The adolescent improves his capacity to think abstractly, can hypothesize, and imagine what might occur instead of being limited by what is. Unlike the child in the concrete operational period, whose thinking depends on the availability of concrete materials, the adolescent deals with objects and relationships by means of symbols, i.e. in the absence of concrete materials. His hypotheses are complex ones, taking into account all eventualities, and exhausting all possible solutions to a problem. He is now capable of logical thinking; he can make inferences, reason inductively and deductively. He uses his imagination in solving problems. Thus, the major difference between the formal operational period and the earlier periods is that the adolescent is now capable of rigorous reasoning in all areas.

The words *period* and *stage* are not synonymous, although they are sometimes used interchangeably. In this guide they refer to two different ideas. The word *period* refers to a large, developmental epoch, as outlined above. The word *stage* refers to a particular concept. Using a chronological point of view, one can speak of a beginning (Stage I), a transitional level (Stage II), and a completion (Stage III) in the acquisition of a particular concept. For example, it is obvious that early in life the child has no notion of what, "to be alive" means. It is likely that he learns the word before it has much meaning to him. During the beginning level, or Stage I, associations to the word are slowly acquired by means of the child's contacts with human beings, animals, television shows, books, etc. On the basis of his limited experiences as well as his limited comprehension, at approximately four years of age, he might define "alive" as, "like when you play ball" or, "like a lady bug." At the next level, Stage II, the transitional stage, the child has taken significant steps toward to the comprehension of the concept "alive" without having mastered it. Six-year-olds, for example, may define it as, "it moves, has a heart and a tail and it can breathe." The Stage II child is on the way toward establishing criteria for "alive," i.e. the definition is more than an association. The completion, the full comprehension of the concept, is referred to as Stage III. With the concept "alive" the child may indicate that he is aware of the differences between animate and inanimate things, between alive and dead beings, that "alive" relates to growth, ability to reproduce, etc.*

The tasks in this manual are primarily useful for ages four to eleven; they focus on the latter part of the preoperational period (the intuitive subperiod) and the concrete operational period.

*See page 68.

To aid the experimenter in summarizing the obtained data, two charts are included.

1. An Individual Profile Chart which provides a visual comparison of the stages of individual concepts for one child.
2. A Group Profile Chart which summarizes the stages of individual concepts for a group of children.

Operations

Piaget defines an *operation* as an internalized action. In his view, the infant's simple actions of looking, kicking, grasping, etc. furnish the basis for later operations. As the child grows older, these actions are repeated many times until they finally become internally represented. This means that at a more mature age one can think about an action without actually performing it. To illustrate, we can think 1 + 1 = 2 without actually manipulating two objects.

An operation has the additional characteristic of being reversible. It can be performed in both directions, as in adding and subtracting, in joining and separating. Reversibility becomes automatic and we take for granted, for example, that numbers added can be subtracted, objects joined in a category can be separated again and placed into other categories, etc.

Piaget has suggested that, as a rule of thumb, many operations may be expressed in common mathematical symbols, such as +, −, x, ÷, >, <, etc.

An operation is never isolated, but always linked to other operations. Different operations form systems. As the child gradually comes to understand their relatedness, his judgments become more stable. This is illustrated by the relatedness of concepts basic to the understanding of mathematics; the operations of multiplication and division become linked to the operations of addition and subtraction.

Operations begin to develop during the intuitive subperiod, but are not immediately coordinated. For example, understanding the operation of addition may precede the understanding of subtraction, and both certainly precede multiplication and division. Slowly operations become coordinated into an organized network of related acts.

From a Piagetian point of view, cognitive development is a process of organization, the elements of which are individual operations. The study of their organization into systems is a major theme in the study of the development of the human mind.

Egocentrism and the Acquisition of Concepts

One of Piaget's most important concepts is *egocentrism,* which helps explain many of the child's misconceptions. The word literally means that the self is the center of the universe and is popularly used to convey selfishness. Piaget assigns it a special meaning; egocentrism refers to the child's inability to place himself in the position of another, to play the role of another, or to see the world from another's perspective.

The process of the discovery of reality is necessarily affected by the child's egocentrism. Since he believes he is the center of his universe, he responds only to his own needs and his own perceptions. He does not understand the difference between cause and effect, between subjective and objective, between dreams and reality. He may consider himself capable of performing such feats as being in two places at the same time, of communicating with inanimate objects, etc. A nursery school child, for example, frequently misapprehends his exact place in the family or social group as well as the limits of his power. He does not accurately understand his relationship to his parents, nor his place in the community or larger society. Although we often assume that children assign the same meaning to words as we do, questioning reveals that children use words egocentrically, that is, with idiosyncratic and private meanings, based on their experience only.*

Egocentrism decreases with increasing age. During the first two years of life the child confuses his own activity with that of the external world. His major task is to differentiate himself by establishing a boundary between himself and the rest of the world. Language plays a major role in the decrease of egocentrism. The

---

*A four-year-old, for example, who was asked what the word *marriage* meant, replied "It means that now your name is Rappaport."

child who is able to discuss issues with his peers compares his own egocentric views of the world with the views of others. In the course of such discussions, new perspectives open up and permit the child a clearer view of the world. Slowly, inaccurate egocentric notions are abandoned in favor of views more closely approximating reality.

Thus the construction of reality is a slow process, spanning the years from birth through adolescence. Most of us do not realize that our adult concepts of the world were actually developed over many years in the course of varied interactions with people, things, and ideas, and that this construction of reality was far from effortless.

Piaget's Clinical Method

Piaget's *clinical method* consists of informal questioning and observation of children. A prepared outline guides the questioner in his explorations of children's ideas. The questioner, or experimenter, need not rigidly adhere to the formal outline in his probing and is encouraged to allow the child's answer to influence, but not to determine, the course of the questioning. In order not to rely exclusively on language, Piaget often provides the child with concrete, manipulable materials to supplement the questioning.

The clinical method has pitfalls of which the beginning experimenter should be aware. Piaget has stated that practice is necessary before passing the inevitable fumbling stage of the beginner.

> It is so hard not to talk too much when questioning a child, especially for an educator; it is so hard not to be suggestive! And above all it is so hard to find a middle course between systematization due to preconceived ideas and incoherence due to the absence of any directing hypothesis. The good experimenter must . . . know how to observe, that is, to let the child talk freely, without ever checking or sidetracking his utterances and at the same time, he must constantly be alert for something definitive; at every moment he must have some working hypothesis, some theory, true or false, which he is seeking to check. When students begin, they either suggest to the child all they hope to find, or they suggest nothing at all, because they are not on the lookout for anything . . .

Additional cautions are in order. It is important to realize that the child's verbalizations often do not reflect his convictions. At times the child creates a myth, a fanciful story, or is led by his imagination into whimsical elaborations. In all cases, thorough and exhaustive questioning is essential.

The type of question used often influences the answers. For example, very young children may sometimes respond to an experimenter's question by repeating the last part. To the question "Which is bigger, or are they both equal?" a child may respond by repeating, "equal." The inexperienced experimenter runs the risk of believing the child to have answered correctly when he has merely parroted a phrase. On the other hand, should the experimenter ask a one-part question, "Which is bigger?" an obedient and conformist child may respond that either one or the other is bigger, despite a suspicion he dares not voice, that the two amounts are really equal.

To explore the development of concepts takes time, skillful questioning, and much devotion, but proves rewarding as it permits adults to tune in to children's thinking. Our interactions with children will become more effective as we match our conversation or teaching to their levels of thinking.

Chapter 2

EXPERIMENTS

INSTRUCTIONS

THE tasks themselves should not be viewed as similar to intelligence tests, but rather as systematic guides to an understanding of the child's acquisition and development of ideas about his world.

Beginning experimenters should first administer the tasks to each other in order to gain proficiency before working with children. In all cases, the children's responses should be recorded verbatim. Nothing should be assumed, and should a response be unclear, additional questions should be asked. The aim of administering the task is to gain information about the child's ideas, not merely to follow the prepared instructions. At the same time, care must be taken not to lead the child into giving the responses which the experimenter considers to be correct. The goal is to determine the level of the child's thought and not to teach a particular concept.

The children's responses to the tasks and questions may be classified according to whether or not they have acquired the concept under observation. You will note that, for each task, criteria are stated which refer to the particular concept explored by the task.

CONSERVATION

Piaget cites a friend's childhood experience. . . . .

> At the age of about 4 or 5 years, he was seated on the ground counting pebbles. He put them in a row and counted them; 1, 2, 3, 4, up to 10. Then he started to count them in the other direction. He began at the end and once again found that he had 10. He found this marvelous . . . so he put them in a circle and counted them that way and found 10 once again . . .

For Piaget, acquisition of the concept of conservation is a major milestone in the development of logical thought. One type of conservation, conservation of substance, was illustrated earlier. Conservation is defined as the concept that certain properties of a substance, such as quantity, remain the same, are invariant, are *conserved,* despite transformations. A substance may be transformed, or undergo a change, as in shape, which alters its appearance, and yet its quantity remains the same. In addition to conservation of substance, there are several different types of conservation. Conservation of weight is illustrated by the question: Which is heavier, a pound of feathers or a pound of lead? A pound remains a pound despite differences in visual image and number of elements, such as feathers. Conservation of volume refers to displacement. A glass container with water in it is used as the common measure. The experimenter shows that two equal balls of clay, when placed in the container, will each cause the water level to rise to the same height. He then alters one of the balls and asks if it will still make the water rise to the same height.

The example which follows illustrates conservation of number. The experimenter arranges a series of sticks in two rows in front of the child and asks if the rows are equal.

After both experimenter and child agree that the number of sticks in the rows are equal, the experimenter transforms one row of sticks, while the other row is left intact.

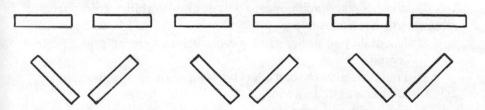

The child is asked whether the number of sticks in the two rows is equal. If the child states that the number of sticks is equal, regardless of their changed appearance, and can explain why, the child has acquired the concept of conservation of number.

Stages of Acquisition

Each conservation concept follows the same developmental trend:

1. Absence of conservation.
2. A transitional period, in which the child's responses are determined mainly by the appearance of the material. Judgments are unpredictable and unstable, because the child has not mastered the principle that if nothing was added or taken away, the amount must remain the same. Conservation may or may not appear in regard to particular materials at this stage.
3. The stage of true conservation, in which the child readily and logically demonstrates understanding of invariant properties (substance, weight, volume) despite transformations of materials.

Despite the similarity in stages of acquisition, not all conservation concepts develop at the same time. Different conservation concepts are acquired at different times, but follow an invariant sequence:

Conservation of substance	Ages 8 to 10
Conservation of weight	Ages 10 to 12
Conservation of volume	Ages 12 and up

Underlying Concepts

Basic concepts which appear to underlie the ability to recognize conservation are as follows:

1. The ability to understand words such as "more," "less," and "equal."
2. The capacity to consider two dimensions simultaneously, such as length and width.
3. The ability to comprehend the whole as composed of parts

which may change their relationship to each other without changing the whole. Height may compensate for width, for example, or width for height; $8 = 1 + 7, 2 + 6$, etc.

4. Reversibility, or the ability to follow a line of reasoning back to where it started, or to follow a series of transformations back to the original state. For example, a child who thinks reversibly, while pouring liquid from a glass into a bowl, can think back to the original water level of the liquid.

Our first task, conservation of number, includes three protocols which illustrate the process of recording the child's verbalizations as well as the three different stages of acquisition of the concept.

* * *

Question: Does the child understand the concept of *conservation of number?*

Task I: One-to-one correspondence in comparing two *equal* sets of objects.

Materials: 6 cups, 6 saucers or 6 glasses, 6 straws.

Instructions:

Establishing Equality

E: Take as many cups as you need so that you will have just one cup for each saucer.

Transformation A

(Take the cups away from saucers and put them in a bunch.)

E: Now do you have as many cups as saucers?

(Return to original position.)

Transformation B

(Spread the saucers out, putting cups in the spaces between the saucers.)

E: Now do you have the same number of cups as saucers?

(Return to original position.)

Transformation C

(Place the cups in two rows of three with the saucers bunched in front.)

E: Now do you have the same number of cups as saucers?
(Return to original position.)

Transformation D

(Place the cups in one long row.)
E: Now do you have the same number of cups as you do saucers?
(Return to original position.)

Analysis

Stage I: under five years
Child makes a rough visual approximation — makes a row of about the same length as the model. Length of one row may be the same, but not the number of items.

Stage II: five to six years
Child places one object opposite each one in the model row and reproduces it exactly without counting; he cannot maintain the concept when the configuration is changed (lacks reversibility).

Stage III: seven to eight years
True conservation. Equality is maintained even after the visual correspondence is altered. Child can act according to principles of logic and is not sidetracked by appearance of materials.

Following are three protocols including sample responses in each of the three stages.

Protocol One

Alison — 4;6*
(Six cups and six saucers were presented to the child.)
E: Take just as many cups as you need, so that you will have one cup for each saucer.

(Alison places a cup on each saucer.)

---
*Four years, six months.

> *Do you have as many cups as you need?*

Alison: *I have a cup for each saucer.*

E: (Takes cups off saucers and puts them in a bunch.) *Now, do you have as many cups as saucers?*

Alison: *I have more cups.*

E: (Spreads cups out, putting a saucer in the space between the cups.) *Now do you have the same number of cups as saucers?*

Alison: *I have more cups because this cup sticks out more than the saucers.*

E: (Places the cups in two rows of three with the saucers bunched in front.)
Now do you have the same number of cups as saucers?

Alison: *I think I have more cups. The cups are a bigger pile.*

E: (Places the cups in one long row.) *Now do you have the same number of cups as you do saucers?*

Alison: *More cups, because they are longer.*

Analysis

Alison is in Stage I. She does not conserve, i.e. she believes that the change of position changes the number of cups or saucers.

Protocol Two

Roger — 6;5

Roger: (Lines up six cups by the saucers when asked by the experimenter to take one cup for each saucer.)

E: *Are you sure that's right?*

Roger: *Yes.*

E: *To make sure you're right, put one cup on one saucer.*

Roger: (Puts cups into saucers, and enjoys the clinking sound.)

E: *Were you right?*

Roger: *Uh-huh.*

E: *Let's take them out* (clusters the cups). *Are there more cups or saucers?*

Roger: He counts the cups.) *The same.*

E: *How do you know?*

Roger: Because there are six.
E: (He clusters the saucers.) *Do I have more cups or saucers now?*
Roger: (He counts again.) *Both the same still.*
E: *But you counted them. Why did you count them?*
Roger: *No, I wasn't sure at first.*

Analysis

Roger is in Stage II. He demonstrates behavior typical of the child in the transitional stage. He appears to conserve, but he is not *certain* that the cups and saucers remain equal in number with changes in position. Each time he has to count the cups in order to be sure. The child who conserves may sometimes count to prove that both sets are equal, but the child in the transitional stage counts because he lacks certainty.

Protocol Three

Julie — 6;7

E: *Take as many cups as you need, so that you will have just one cup for each saucer.* (Julie puts a cup into each saucer.)
Julie: *I have six cups and six saucers.*
E: (Takes the cups and puts them in a bunch.) *Now do you have the same number of cups as saucers?*
Julie: *Yes, there are still six cups and six saucers.*
E: (Spreads out cups, putting a saucer between each cup.) *Now do you have the same number of cups as saucers?*
Julie: *Yes, because you didn't take any cups or saucers away.*
E: (Places the cups in two rows of three with the saucers bunched in front.) *Now do you have the same number of cups as saucers?*
Julie: *Yes, because I have three cups and three cups and that's six, and you didn't take any saucers away.*
E: (Places the cups in one long row.) *Now do you have the same number of saucers as you do cups?*
Julie: *Yes, because you still have the same cups and saucers.*

You just mixed them up. (This reasoning held up no matter how the cups or saucers were arranged.)

Analysis

Julie is in Stage III. She understands conservation of number, i.e. she is certain that amounts remain unchanged and is able to give reasons for her belief, such as "you didn't take any cups away." Julie demonstrates behavior typical of a child in the concrete operational stage.

* * *

Question: **Does the child understand the concept of** *conservation of number?**

Task II: One-to-one correspondence in comparing two *unequal* sets of objects.

Materials: 8 chips or checkers of one color
10 chips or checkers of another color

Instructions:

Transformation A

(Place *eight* chips of one color in a row and give child a pile of *ten* chips of another color.)

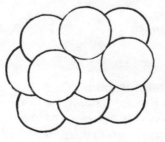

---

*This task is similar to the previous one and is included to enable the experimenter to compare the child's responses to the same task with the use of different materials.

E: *Will you please fix these chips so that you are sure you have just as many chips as I have?* (If child does not lay out an equal number of chips in a matching row, note this and note how child did attempt to determine equality. Then suggest that a matching row be constructed.)

Transformation B

E: *Now we both have the same number of chips. Watch what I'm going to do.* (Gather up first row of chips and lay them out in a small circle.)

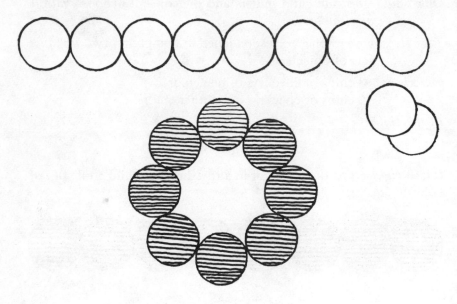

E: *Now who has more chips?*
E: *Why?*

Transformation C

(Return chips to two matching rows before moving to next transformation. Follow same procedure with each transformation.)

E: Now watch what I am going to do. (Spread chips out in a long line. See task immediately preceding for other transformations.)

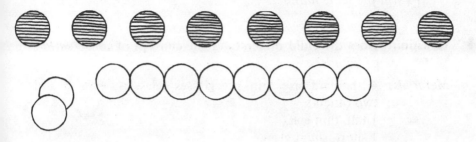

Analysis

Stage I: under five years

Child makes a rough visual approximation and often makes a row of about the same length as the model. Length of row may be the same, but not the number of items.

Stage I Sample Responses

C: * *There are more in this line because it's bigger.*
There are more here because it's not spread out.
There are less here because there's a bundle.

Stage II: five to six years

Child places one object opposite each one in the model row and reproduces it exactly without counting; he cannot maintain the concept when the configuration is changed (lacks reversibility).

Stage II Sample Responses

C: There are more here because I have one left over.
You can see by the line there aren't as many here.

Stage III: seven to eight years

True conservation: Equality is maintained even after the visual correspondence is altered. Child can act according to principles of logic and is not sidetracked by appearance of materials.

---

*C signifies child.

Stage III Sample Responses

C: You've only moved them around; it's still the same.
You didn't add anything or take anything away.
It's still the same number.

* * *

Question: **Does the child understand the concept of** *conservation*
of liquids?

Materials: 4 standard size drinking glasses (glass A, glass B and
two others)
1 tall, thin glass
1 short, squat glass
4 small identical glasses
colored liquids or juice

Instructions:

Transformation A

(Fill two standard glasses, glass A and glass B, with liquid)

E: This is my glass (A) *and this is your glass* (B).
E: Do we both have the same amount of juice (soda, water, etc.)?

(Note how the child decides equality. Let him adjust amounts
if he so desires. He must agree that amounts are equal before
task is continued.)

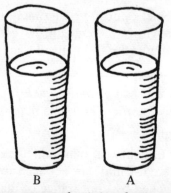

B   A

E: Now I'm going to pour the juice from my glass (A) *into this*
glass (tall, thin). *Now which has more juice, this glass* (B) *or*
the tall, thin glass? Or are they both the same?

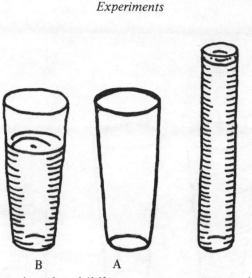

B   A

E: *Why?* (Question the child's response no matter what it is.)

E: *Now I'll pour my juice back into this glass* (A).
   Who has more juice now, or do we both have the same?

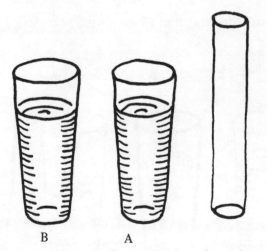

B   A

(Follow the same pattern of questioning through the following transformations.)

Transformation B

E pours juice from standard Glass A into short, squat glass.

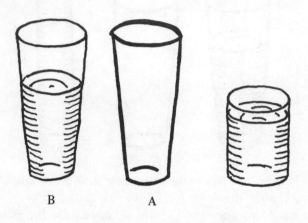

B   A

Transformation C

E pours juice from standard Glass A into two glasses the same size as Glass A.

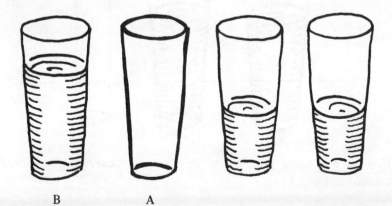

B   A

Transformation D

E pours juice into four small glasses.

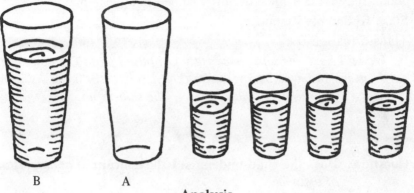

B   A

Analysis

Stage I: four to six years

The child cannot deal with two dimensions such as height and width. He states that the amount of liquid changes as it appears different when the level changes in different containers.

Stage I Sample Responses

Transformation A

C: This one is more. I can see it's higher.

Transformation C

C: You have more to drink because you have two glasses and I have one. The juice is getting tired.

Stage II: six to eight years

Transitional. The child sometimes appears to conserve, but usually focuses either on height or on width and becomes confused with questioning.

Stage II Sample Responses

Transformation D

C: You have more glasses and I only have one. You have more. (Realizes another possibility) *We have the same. Your glass is just a different shape.*

Stage III: eight years and up

Child consistently realizes that an increase or a decrease in height or width is compensated for. If the amounts were originally equal, they remain equal despite changes in appearance.

Stage III Sample Responses

Transformation D

C: *We still have the same because you poured from the same glass as mine and we had the same then, so we still have the same now. The four glasses have to have the same amount as the one glass.*

* * *

Question: **Does the child understand the concept of** *conservation of distance?*

Materials: 2 plastic toys, such as cowboys, soldiers, etc. 2 to 3 inches in height.

1 cardboard screen higher than the toys

1 cardboard screen lower than the toys

1 block of wood, about 2 inches wide and 1 inch high

Instructions:

Part I: Place the two toys on a table about twenty inches apart. Ask the child if he thinks the toys are "near together" or "far apart." When he responds, place the high screen halfway between the figures and ask if the figures are still as near or as far apart, depending on the child's first reply.

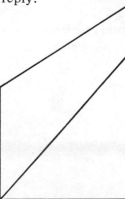

If the child believes that the screen changed the distance between the two figures, ask why.

Part II: Same procedure with the low screen.

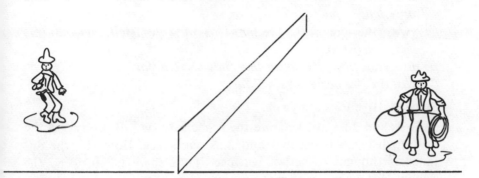

Part III: Same procedure with the wooden block.

 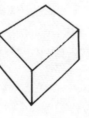 

Analysis

Stage I: under five years

The introduction of a screen changes the distance relationship between the two toys. The child cannot deal with one distance broken into two parts. He perceives two distances, one from each toy to the screen. He now considers a part of the whole with which he began and finds that the distance is less or more; he states that the toys are "nearer than they were before," or that they are "further away."

Stage I Sample Responses

C: It's further when the screen isn't there because when it is, it's only half as far.

C: (with the screen) *It's less far. This one is by itself, and that one is by itself too.*

E: But aren't they far apart like they were before?

C: No, they're nearer the screen.

Stage II: five to seven years

The child does not separate the space into two. He considers the overall distance between 1 and 2 as one space. However, the distance is thought to be less because of the space taken up by the screen. Distance means empty space.

Stage II Sample Responses

C: It isn't far because there's a wall.

They're still far apart except for one tiny bit there where the screen is.

It's nearer; it (the screen) separates them.

Stage III; seven years and up

The distance is conserved regardless of the objects between the toys.

Stage III Sample Responses

C: It's as far as it was.

It doesn't make any difference when there's a screen.

It's always the same because this screen can't make them move.

* * *

Question: **Does the child understand the concept of** *conservation of area?*

Task I: Abstract shapes

Material: Two cardboard or construction paper rectangles, each made up of 6 squares of equal size.

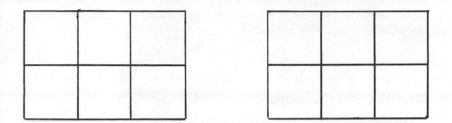

Instructions:

(Place both rectangles before the child.)

E: Are these two rectangles the same size? Do they take up the same amount of room? (Note how the child determines equality. Then transfer top right hand square of one rectangle to bottom left hand corner.)

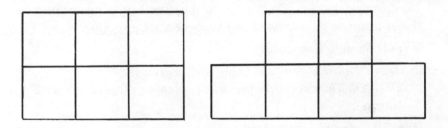

E: Do they take up the same amount of room now? Why? (Replace in original position and move another square.)

Alternate or additional variations:

Use the same procedure with two rectangles, one of which is cut into two triangles.

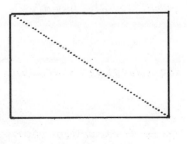

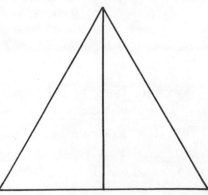

With nonconservers or transitional-stage children, try the triangle in the inverted position to see whether the child changes his mind about which figure is larger.

Analysis

Stage I: under five years

No conservation. The child judges on the basis of appearance. When appearance is modified or the whole is sectioned into parts, area is not conserved.

Stage I Sample Responses

C: They're not the same; this one's bigger (points to original rectangle). *This one takes up less room because it goes like this* (traces outline of original rectangle).

Stage II: six to seven years

Transitional stage. Child tries to measure but is uncertain how. Makes intuitive adjustments but lacks general principle.

Stage II Sample Responses

C: There's more room here (points to rectangle).
Oh NO! They're both the same, I think. (measures with his fingers).

Stage III: seven years and up

True conservation; child does not lose concept when shapes are altered or sectioned into parts.

Stage III Sample Responses

C: It's the same room because it's the same squares. It looked bigger at the bottom and I remembered it was the same squares. You simply turned it around differently, but it's the same size as before.

* * *

Question: Does the child understand the concept of *conservation of area?*

Task II: Representational items

Materials: Two identical sheets of green construction paper, approximately 12" x 18 ", 2 small toy cows, 20 small blocks of equal size.

Instructions:

E: Let's pretend that these pieces of paper are two fields of grass. Each cow has her own field. Do both cows have the same amount of grass to eat?

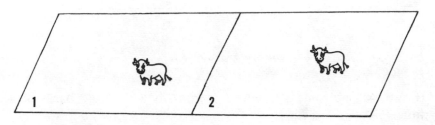

(Note how child determines that two fields are equal in size.)

E: Let's make believe these blocks are barns. Now I'll put a barn (block) *in one field. Which cow has more grass to eat?*

E: Why?

(If child suggests that the barn contains food, say that it does not.)

E: Now we'll add a barn to this other field. Do both cows have the same amount to eat now?

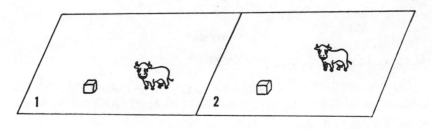

E: Now I'll put another barn on each field.

(Place second barn so that one touches the first barn on one field, but is separated from the first barn on the other field.)

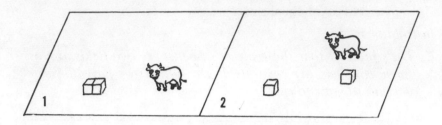

E: Now which cow has more grass to eat?
E: Why?

(Continue the same procedure, adding one or more barns at a
time.)

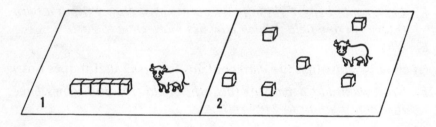

Analysis

Stage I: under five years

No conservation. The child believes the area is changed with the
placement of the barns, either together or apart from one another.

Stage I Sample Responses

(Barn is placed on both fields in same position.)
C: Yes, it's the same.
(Barns are placed in different positions; one at the edge.)
C: No, there's more grass here (one at edge).
E: Why?

C: Because there is all this left (empty space).
(Two barns on one field, 1 barn on second.)
C: There is more left on this one.
(Two barns together in a corner on 1 field, 2 barns spread apart on other field)
C: No, there's more green left here (Field 2).
E: Why?
C: Because these houses are touching and there is lots of grass left.
As experimenter adds more barns, the child responds that there is more grass on one field than on the other.

Stage II: five to seven years

Transitional. Child recognizes that grass areas are equal as long as arrangement of barns is identical. As the number of barns increases, it becomes more difficult to retain the concept of conservation.

Stage II Sample Responses

(One barn on Field 1.)
C: Both cows don't have the same to eat because the barn takes up room.
(One barn on each field.)
C: Both cows have the same to eat.
E: Why?
C: Because both are the same size.
(Two barns on each field. Close together on Field 1, far apart on field 2.)
C: That one has more to eat. (Field 2).
E: Why?
C: Not that one (1). *No, that one* (2).
(Three barns close together on Field 1, three barns far apart on Field 2.)
C: (Begins to count barns.) *The same.*
E: Why?
C: The barns are the same.

Stage III: above seven years

True conservation. Child recognizes that the remaining area is always equal despite the seeming disparity; adding or subtracting equal numbers must result in equal areas.

Stage III Sample Responses

(Four barns are touching on Field 1, scattered on Field 2.)

C: They still have the same, because the barns still take up the same amount of space.

(Add 5 barns to each field.)

C: Let me see. They have the same because the barns still take up the same amount of space even if they are together.

* * *

Question: **Does the child understand the concept of** *conservation of weight?*

Materials: Two balls of clay, equal in size and weight
Scale

Instructions:

(Place two equal clay balls in front of the child.)

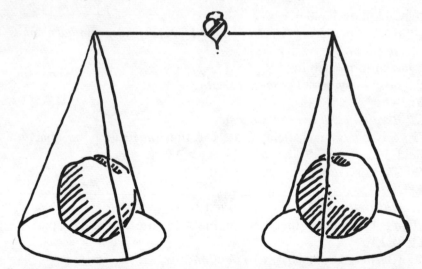

E: Do they both weigh the same? Do they both have the same amount of weight, or is one as heavy as the other?

(Place the balls on the scale so the child can see they weigh the same. Remove the balls from scale. Transform one ball into a sausage shape.)

E: Will they weigh the same now, or will one be heavier?

(Other transformations may be added.)

Analysis

Stage I: five to seven years

No conservation. Child judges by a single dimension. Usually the sausage shape is judged heavier than the ball because it's longer.

Stage I Sample Responses

C: This sausage has more weight in it.
E: Why?
C: Can't you see it's longer?

Stage II: seven to nine years

The child vacillates between the two dimensions involved. He sometimes believes the ball is heavier because it's wider, and at other times believes the sausage is heavier because it's longer.

Stage II Sample Responses

C: I guess this one will weigh more because it has more clay in it (sausage). *But maybe we can make the other one into this shape, and then it will weigh the same.*

Stage III: ten years and up

True conservation; the child can consider both dimensions and come to the correct conclusion.

Stage III Sample Responses

C: You just changed the shape of it, that's all, so the weight will still be the same. You didn't add anything that would make it heavier.

* * *

Question: **Does the child understand the concept of** *conservation of volume?*

Materials: A house built of 36 blocks, 1 cubic inch each, built on a cardboard base (1), measuring 3 x 4 (thus, height would be 3 blocks)
36 blocks unassembled
cardboard base (2) measuring 2 x 3

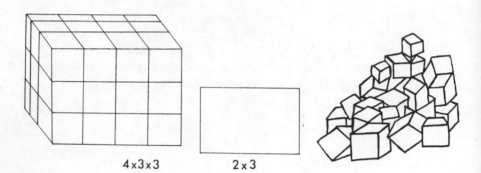

4 x 3 x 3   2 x 3

Instructions:

Show child the house on Base 1. Tell him it is necessary to build a new house on a different plot of land. The new house has to have as much room in it as the first house, although its shape may be different. Be sure to stress that the *amount of room* in the house is what is important, not the shape of the house.

Analysis

Stage I: four to seven years

Comparisons are made in terms of one dimension only. For instance, child may refuse to build a taller house to allow for the decrease in size of the base. Model is compared as "bigger," "thicker," or "thinner."

Stage I Sample Responses

(The child builds a house of equal height as model.)

E: Is that enough?

C: *Yes, that's enough.*

E: *Which is bigger?* (Child points to model) *Is there the same amount of room in it?*

C: *It's the same because it's just as tall.*

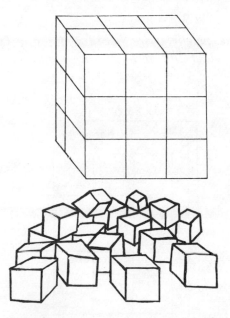

Stage II: six to twelve years

Child begins to work out relations between the three dimensions; now builds a taller house but cannot determine just how much taller it should be; makes a number of trial and error attempts.

Stage II Sample Responses

(The child builds the same height as model.)

C: *I don't know how to finish. Oh yes, I have to make it higher — now there's enough* (adds another story).

E: *Look carefully* (child adds another story).

C: *This time I think it's right.*

E: *Why?*

C: *I have to make it higher because I can't make it any thicker.*

Stage III: over twelve years of age

Child can now make numerical computations; he discovers the

relationship between area and volume (two volumes are equal if the products of their lengths in three dimensions are equal, or length x width x height = volume).

Stage III Sample Responses

(The child builds a 2 x 3 x 6 house.)

C: I've made the height more because this one (model) *is less high, but it's wider and mine is thinner and narrower, but it's higher.*

3x2x6

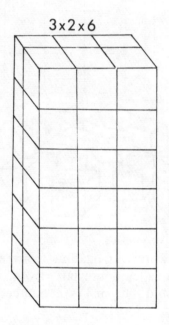

CLASSIFICATION

Much of our commerce with the environment involves dealing with classes of things rather than with unique events and objects. Indeed the case can be made that all cognitive activity depends upon a prior placing of events in terms of their category membership.

Jerome Bruner

The ability to classify appears in children in adult-like forms by the age of about eight. How does the child learn to classify? It is an ability which develops in preschool age children and thus is not a "taught" school subject. Therefore, is it learned by the child on her own? If we study the development of classification, can we perhaps find more general answers to the question of how children learn on their own?

How do we test the development of the concept of "class"? Suppose an experimenter presents a child with a mixed collection of red and blue chips. The older child may first think of the chips as members of classes: *the class of red chips* and the *class of blue chips.* In addition, she may realize that the *class of red chips,* for example, is a subclass and is included in a larger class, that of *chips in general.* Thus, as she groups the red chips into a class, she may conceive of them as part of a hierarchy of classes: the class larger than the *red chips* is the class of *chips in general.* In turn, the class of *chips in general* is a subclass which is included in the class of *solid objects.*

Young children frequently lack the idea of class inclusion despite the fact that they use words which, to adults, suggest that they do understand it. For example, to adults the word "car" stands for the class of vehicles composed of various types (station wagon, convertible, sedan, etc.) and of various makes.

Lucy, a three-year-old, constructed a classification system in which there are only subclasses: VW's, campers, station wagons, buses, trucks, Fords, and "cars." "Cars" to her are all those cars or trucks she has not as yet differentiated.

Developmental Stages

Infancy: According to Piaget, early forms of classification appear in infancy as classes are constructed on the basis of the child's interaction with objects in her environment. For example, an infant who sucks everything will categorize things as either suckable or not. Such early forms of classification are practical classifications, or classification-in-action, since the infant learns the properties of objects on the basis of her activities with them. With the passage of time, she refines her simple classification system by adjusting her actions to the objects. For example, she may classify objects she has placed in her mouth according to hardness (a key), or softness (a marshmallow). A new object may evoke a series of actions, such as sucking, touching, banging, and it often seems that the infant performs these actions in an attempt to include the object in a class of objects already known to her. Such simple forms of classification-in-action exist before the development of language.

Up to five years: The preschool child seems to group objects according to personal associations rather than abstract and objective criteria. At this age, characteristically, the child appears to take each step in her sorting as she comes to it; she does not have an overall plan, such as sorting according to similarities and differences of objects. She frequently appears to forget what she has actually begun to do. There appears to be no goal to her sorting; criteria, when first used, are ephemeral and constantly change. For example, a child may set out to align red circles, switch to red triangles, then switch to green triangles, after which she will change to some other criterion. Frequently, color, shape, or size of one object seem to suggest the next step. At some point in the sorting, the child may announce that she is building a house, bridge, or plane, etc. thus adding a graphic or representational element to her collections. Since these groups are not established on the basis of abstract characteristics such as similarities or differences, they are not *classes*. They might be called *collections*. Because the groups represent something, or have a theme, the stage is referred to as the stage of *graphic collections*.

Six to eight years: The next stage in the development of classification concepts is referred to as the *nongraphic collection*, and is viewed as a transitional stage. Typical of this stage is the assignment of objects to one collection or another on the basis of visual similarity alone. Although this arrangement is no longer graphic or representational, it is not yet based on abstract characteristics and thus is not a true class. The several collections are not arranged according to hierarchical class structure but are simply placed next to one another. Hierarchical class structure means that Class A includes and is larger than Class B which includes and is larger than Class C (A>B>C). For example, the class of solid objects (A) includes the class of chips (B) which includes the class of red chips (C). This notion of class inclusion appears to be absent until about the age of eight.

Eight years and up: True classification appears. The child is able to understand class inclusion; that is, she comprehends the relationship of classes to subclasses.

A note of caution: Behaviorally, the stage of true classification may not be distinguishable from the nongraphic collection, at least as far as the sorting of concrete materials is concerned. Since materials can be sorted in space only, one cannot be sure whether the child sorts according to the similarities of the materials alone, or whether the notion of class inclusion is present. The determination of the presence or absence of class inclusion in a child's thinking requires a verbal task, directions for which appear elsewhere in this guide. The verbal task is necessary to elicit the existence of the idea of class inclusion, since the arrangement of the elements in a sorting task may be the same for both stages, namely the nongraphic collection and the true classification. The verbal task deals with the hierarchical structure of classes.

* * *

Question: Can the child *spontaneously classify geometric objects?*

Materials: 6 circles
6 squares
6 triangles
6 rectangles
(All shapes made of wood, plastic, or cardboard of 3 different colors.)

Instructions:

Present shapes in random array.

Tell child to put together the things that go together, put together the things that are the same or put the things in order.

Analysis

Stage I: under five years

The child has no plan as to the goal of sorting; criteria are not held in mind and constantly change. The child may start by aligning six rectangles, the last of which is yellow. Then she may select two yellow triangles, followed by two yellow circles. This in turn leads to four circles of other colors. Either the color or the shape of the last item used seems to determine the next choice.

Sorting sometimes turns into object representation, such as building a bridge or a tower (graphic collection). Some objects are usually left unclassified.

Stage I Sample Responses

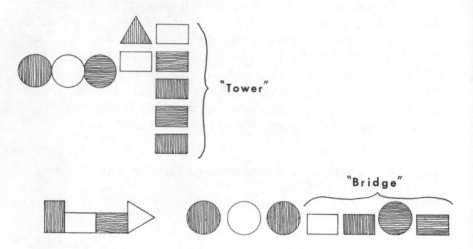

"Tower"

"Bridge"

Stage II: five to seven years

Perceptual similarity, such as shape, color, or both, is used as a basis for sorting. Sometimes the child seems to form classes; however, collections are juxtaposed and not seen in true relation to each other. All objects are usually used up, in contrast to Stage I. Most important is that the child does not yet understand the relationship among different levels of a class hierarchy.

Stage II Sample Responses

The shapes are classified according to either shape or color.

(blue) (red) (yellow)

Stage III: eight years and up

True classification, the child demonstrates an overall conceptual plan in the hierarchical arrangements of classes.

Stage III Sample Responses

The child makes up classes based on shape, as well as subclasses based on colors, or vice versa, and comprehends the hierarchical relationship.

One cannot be certain whether the child sorts according to Stage II or Stage III criteria on the basis of observation alone. A verbal task on class inclusion should be used (see Classification of Animals).

* * *

Question: Can the child *spontaneously classify representational objects?*

Materials: Toy array consisting of two or more

people	cars
houses	babies
animals	cradles
trees	pots, pans

(Varied materials such as wood, plastic, etc. should be used. Note that toys should not be presented in any special order.)

In contrast to the previous task, neither children nor adults seem to classify the toys. Rather, they construct groups with a theme, such as a village. In order to help the subjects classify, Piaget asked them to place the "same" elements on to separate pieces of paper, to put all the people on one sheet, etc. This procedure is optional. It is important to compare the sorting of the geometric objects with the sorting of the toys. The geometric objects appear to facilitate classification, while the toy-like representational objects lead to play. Thus stage of classification appears to be influenced by the materials to be classified. Representational materials with rich associational meanings are sometimes a hindrance, rather than a help to the learning of classification.

* * *

Question: **Does the child understand the concept of** *class inclusion?*

Does the child understand the concepts *all and some?*

Materials: Shapes cut out of colored construction paper:
2 blue squares
2 red squares
5 blue circles

Instructions:
(Present the following pattern of cutout colored shapes to the child.)

blue | red | blue

E: *Are all the squares red?*
Are all the blue ones circles?
Are all the red ones squares?
Are all the circles blue?

Analysis

Stage I: under four years
The child cannot deal with "all" and "some." She has no concept of class and sorts shapes according to perceptual associations.

Stage I Sample Responses
E: *Are all the squares red?*
C: *These are red, these are blue, and these* (She counts the blue circles, 1, 2, 3, 4, 5).
E: *Why?*
C: *'Cause there are two of them.*
E: *Are all the blue ones circles?*

C: No. Two are squares.
E: Why?
C: 'Cause two are squares.
E: Are all the red ones squares?
C: Yeah.
E: Why?
C: I don't know.
E: Are all the circles blue?
C: (Looks very carefully) *Five of them are.*
E: Why?
C: 'Cause I counted them (Points to the five circles).

Stage II: five to seven years
"All" is not truly a logical concept as yet. Groups are formed according to similarity of appearance.

Stage II Sample Responses
E: Are all the squares red?
C: No.
E: Why?
C: There are red ones and blue ones (correct).
E: Are all the blue ones circles?
C: No.
E: Why?
C: There are blue circles and squares (correct).
E: Are all the red ones squares?
C: Yes (correct).
E: Are all the circles blue?
C: No (incorrect).
E: Why?
C: Because there are blue squares and circles (incorrect).

Stage III: seven years
Child understands class inclusion. The display yields these classes and subclasses.

I. Class of blue objects
    Subclass blue circles
    Subclass blue squares

II. Class of squares
    Subclass blue squares
    Subclass red squares

Stage III Sample Responses
E: Are all the squares red?
C: No.

E: Why?

C: There are blue squares and red ones.

E: Are all the blue ones circles?

C: No.

E: Why?

C: There are some squares and circles that are blue.

E: Are all the red ones squares?

C: Yes.

E: Why?

C: There are only two reds, both are squares.

E: Are all the circles blue?

C: Yes.

E: Why?

C: There are only two red ones and they both are square. Only the blue circles are left.

* * *

Question: Does the child understand the concept of *class inclusion?* **Is the child able to construct classes and subclasses (class hierarchy) using representational objects?**

Materials: 3 ducks   (Class A)
4 other birds, not ducks   (Class B)
3 animals without wings   (Class C)
3 inanimate objects   (Class D)
4 transparent envelopes or boxes of graduated sizes. The smallest should fit into the next larger, etc.
4 labels to be attached to the envelopes or boxes

The classes which define the sequence of inclusion are ducks (Class A), birds (Class B), animals (Class C), and the universal class, all objects (Class D). Therefore, $A<B<C<D$. If the experimenter believes these items are foreign to the experience of the child, alternate pictures should be used.

Instructions:

E: Here are some cards with pictures on them. Here is a＿＿＿＿＿ (child fills in name). Here is a ＿＿＿＿＿(child fills in name). Can you make some piles with animals that are like each other? Find the cards with the same kind of animals and put them together.

E: *Here are some labels that say ducks, birds, and animals. We'll put each label on an envelope.*

E: *This envelope says birds. Can we put these* (ducks) *in here and still keep the same label? Why?* (Correct response: yes.)

E: *This envelope says animals. Can we put these* (birds) *in here and still keep the same label? Why?* (Correct response: yes.)

E: *This envelope says ducks. Can we put these* (birds) *in here and still keep the same label? Why?* (Correct response: no.)

E: *This envelope says birds. Can we put these* (animals) *in here and still keep the same label? Why?* (Correct response: no.)
(Spread out all the cards.)

E: *Are there more ducks than birds? Why?*
Are there more animals than ducks? Why?
Are there more animals than birds? Why?
If all the ducks in the world died, would there be any birds left? Why?
If all the birds in the world died, would there be any ducks left? Why?

E: *If all the animals in the world died, would there be any ducks left? Why?*
   If all the ducks in the world died, would there be any animals left? Why?
   If all the animals in the world died, would there be any birds left? Why?
   If all the birds in the world died, would there be any animals left? Why?

Analysis

Stage I: five to seven years

Child can make spontaneous but not logical classifications. She can separate animals that walk from those that fly, but does not have the notion of class inclusion. For instance, the child will often say that ducks are animals, but is unwilling to place the pictures of ducks in the pile labelled animals.

Stage I Sample Responses

E: *Here are some cards with some pictures of animals and things. Take a look at them all.*

C: *This isn't an animal, it's a car. What's this one?*

E: *That's a clock. Now some of these animals are ducks. Help me pick out the cards that are ducks and we'll put them in the envelope that says ducks on it. That's right. Let's put all the ducks in the duck envelope.*

C: *Okay; they're all in there now.*

E: *Now let's put all the birds in this envelope that says birds. That's right. Pick them all out and put them in the envelope. Do you have them all?*

C: *Yes. There are no birds left on the table.*

E: *Now, let's put all the animals in this envelope marked animals.*

C: *Okay. Oh, the car is left and what is this thing again?*

E: *A clock. Now I'm going to ask you some questions about these cards. If all the animals died, would there be any birds left?*

C: *No.*

E: *If all the birds died, would there be any ducks left?*

C: *Yes.*

Stage II: seven to ten years

Transitional. Beginning of class inclusion is present. For

example, the child will recognize that if all the birds were dead, there would still be animals left.

Stage II Sample Responses

E: (Presenting envelope labelled ducks.) *What do you think we should do now?*

C: *Put all the ducks in there?*

E: *Right. Do it.*

E: (Presenting envelope labelled birds.) *What should we do with this?*

C: *Put all the birds in it.*

E: (Presenting envelope labelled animals.) *Now what?*

C: (Proceeds to put animal pictures in bag, leaving out inanimate objects.)

E: *Can we put the ducks in with the birds?*

C: *Yes, they're both alike.*

E: *Can we put birds in with animals?*

C: *No, birds aren't animals.*

E: *If all the birds died, would we have ducks?*

C: *No.*

E: *Why?*

C: *Birds and ducks, they're the same.*

E: *If all the animals died, would we have birds and ducks?*

C: *No.*

E: *Why?*

C: *Birds and ducks are not humans. They're animals.*

Stage III: nine to eleven years

Child has true notion of class inclusion. She knows that $A < B < C < D$ or that ducks are birds, birds are animals, animals are part of the universal class. Child can also reverse the process, that is, $D > C > B > A$.

Sample III Sample Responses

E: *Here are some cards with some pictures of animals and things. Now some of the cards are ducks. I'm going to put all the cards that are ducks into this envelope that says ducks. Now I'm going to put all the birds in this envelope that says birds. Now let's put all the other animals into the envelope marked animals. Are there any cards left?*

C: Yes, the car and the clock.

E: Right. Now let me ask you some questions. If all the animals died, would there be any birds left?

C: No.

E: If all the birds died, would there be any ducks left?

C: No.

E: If all the ducks died, would there be any birds left?

C: Yes.

E: If all the birds died, would there be any animals left?

C: Yes.

E: If all the animals died, would there be anything left?

C: Yes.

E: What would be left?

C: Anything that wasn't an animal, like things. Like the car and the clock.

* * *

Question: **Can the child classify by more than one criterion? Can the child use** *multiple classification?*

Materials: 1. One row of blue objects drawn on a strip of paper (hat, pumpkin, leaf, pail).
   2. One row of stars in different colors except blue.
   3. Single objects similar to individual objects pictured in (1) and (2), and several stars, one of which is blue.

Instructions:

An empty space is provided at the point of intersection of the two rows of objects. Ask the child to fill in this space using one of a group of pictures shown to her. Only the blue star fits the intersection and is the correct solution. Ask the child to put the picture which "belongs" or "fits," e.g. "What should I put here that will go with all these (point) and all these (point)?"

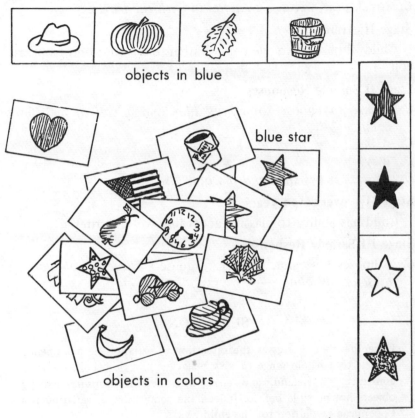

objects in blue

blue star

objects in colors

colored stars

Analysis

Stage I: below six years

Choice is based on one collection; the child matches according to visual impressions such as nearness to another element, color, shape, or other similarity. Objects at the other point of intersection are ignored.

Stage I Sample Responses

C: Pail (closest element).

C: *Brown star* (choice based on shape).

C: *Banana, because they taste good.*

C: *Green pear, because that fits in with the leaves.*

Stage II: (rare)

Child chooses two elements rather than one; one from each collection.

Stage II Sample Responses

C: *I have to choose something blue and a pail of a different color.*

C: *A flag.*

E: *Why?*

C: *Because it has stars and it's blue also.*

Stage III: over seven years

Child has ability to classify according to two criteria.

Stage III Sample Responses

C: (Chooses blue star, correct response.) *These are all stars and these are all blue.*

SERIATION

Once the child possesses the operation of seriation he has opened himself to a whole range of new behaviors . . . . he becomes able to construct, understand, and cope with new relationships among objects not possible before. Indeed the acquisition of seriation is a Copernican revolution for the child.

Jean Piaget

The concept of seriation, or rank ordering, refers to the placing of things in a series. We know that children have acquired the concept of seriation when they can arrange objects in a series according to size, weight, color hue, or other criteria. Children playing with nesting boxes or building towers with blocks of decreasing size appear to learn how to seriate on an action level.

Developmental Stages

Seriation, similar to other operations, is based on actions

carried out by the child early in life. The ability to seriate is acquired gradually, and several levels of development may be observed. Under the age of one, children rarely seriate. During the next few years, they frequently divide items into two categories, such as large or small, light or dark, etc. They do not necessarily order all the elements offered to them. Older children divide objects into finer categories: large, middle-sized, or small; dark, of intermediate darkness, or light, etc. During the transitional stage, children construct series by trial and error and are not able to immediately produce the correct series. Finally, at the most advanced stage, the child invents a method. In seriating according to size, for example, he may choose the largest object, set it aside, choose the largest of the remaining, place it alongside the first, choose the largest of the remaining, etc. until he has ordered all the elements. Each element is smaller than the ones which have gone before it and larger than the ones to follow. A child may, of course, also begin with the smallest element and proceed toward the largest. What is significant here, and what distinguishes this stage from earlier ones, is the existence of a method to accomplish the ordering of elements into series.

* * *

Question: Does the child understand the concept of *seriation?*

Materials: Ten small rods, or strips of cardboard, ranging in length from about 1″ to 10″ all of the same width. Cuisinaire rods may also be used, although rods of one color are preferable.

Instructions:

Present rods in random array.

Part A: Tell the child to arrange the sticks in order. Do not mention size in order to test whether the child will seriate spontaneously.

Present rods in random array.

Part B: Tell the child to arrange the sticks or rods going from the "smallest to the largest" or from the "littlest to the biggest."

Analysis

Stage I: under five years

The child usually divides the rods into two groups, such as large and small.

Stage I Sample Responses

C: These are the big ones and these are the little ones.

C: I have little ones over here; over there the sticks are different.

Stage II: five to six years

   Partial seriation sometimes occurs; the child sometimes divides the sticks into three groups: small, medium, and large. Correct seriation for a few sticks is sometimes shown.

Stage II Sample Responses

C: These are long, these are short, these are almost long, this one is left over.

   The child usually has the first and last right, but confusions are shown with sticks of similar size.

Stage III: seven to eight years

   Child is able to seriate all ten sticks correctly.

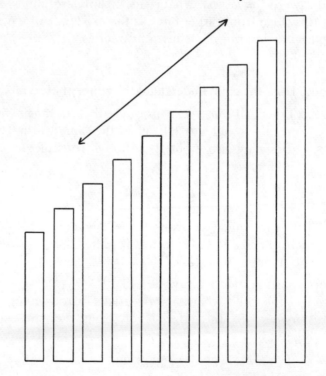

* * *

Questions: Does the child understand the concept of *multiple seriation?* (serial ordering of objects which differ in two respects: e.g. size and color intensity)

Materials: Twenty-five pictures of cars, or other appropriate objects, cut out of paper or cardboard, all alike except for differences in sizes and color intensity.

Instructions:

Present pictures in random array.

Tell the child, "I would like you to order (or put together, or arrange) these cars in the way you think they should go." If the child is unable to construct the series, arrange five cars according to size in a row and five cars according to color intensity in a column; then encourage the child to fill in the rest. A table, or matrix, will result, if the arrangement is correct.

Analysis

Stage I: under five years

No real <u>seriation,</u> but an intermediate ordering between classification and seriation, a "graphic collection."

Stage I Sample Responses

Divides twenty-five elements into a number of collections, some based on size, and some on color. Makes separate stacks for the different colors, not seriated.

C: I'm building a parking lot.

Stage II: five to six years

Seriation, but according to one criterion only, sometimes switching from one to the other. Child may order according to size alone or color alone.

Stage II Sample Responses

Classifies according to five different colors and then takes the lightest color and seriates by size.

Stage III: seven years and over

Seriation according to two criteria.

Stage III Sample Responses

Children realize they will have to seriate according to two criteria as soon as they see the material.

C: Some are darker and some are smaller.
C: I keep looking at the smaller ones and the lighter ones.

CAUSALITY

Piaget's young daughter, seeing the clouds of smoke rising from her father's pipe, assumed that he was responsible for the clouds in the sky and the mists around the mountaintops of Switzerland.

Early in life the child is not able to distinguish between the subjective and the objective, a characteristically egocentric attitude. However, in order to understand cause-and-effect sequences, the child must first establish a boundary between what is private, internal experience and what is objective reality. Piaget studied children's ideas about the differences between subjective and objective states by means of a number of questionnaires, covering such ideas as what makes clouds move, why do some objects sink while others float, what does "alive" mean, etc. He classified their explanations according to whether the children could differentiate between the subjective and the objective and thus had a basis for comprehending cause-and-effect relationships.

In addition to the confusion about objective and subjective reality, children are prone to other confusions as they try to make sense of the world. Since such confusions occur before the understanding of cause-and-effect relationships, they are called *precausal*. There are several types of precausal confusions: *realism, animism, artificialism, dynamism, finalism,* and *phenomenism*.

Realism refers to the tendency to make tangible and objective what is intangible and subjective. Since children often believe that thoughts and dreams are as real as things, they may think that others know their thoughts or see their dreams. They tend to give a false reality and a concrete existence to what is subjective, intangible, and internal (see Concept of Dreams).

Animism refers to a tendency to attribute subjective experience, feelings, consciousness, etc. to objects and events which are inanimate. The belief that a boat feels hurt and is crying, that a house knows who is living in it, are examples of animism (see Concept of Life).

Dynamism is similar to animism; children assume that the same energy and muscle power granted to human beings and animals are also granted to objects and that all things are capable of movement and effort. The story of "The Little Engine that Could" is an example of dynamism (see Floating and Sinking of Objects).

Finalism refers to the precausal tendency to regard nonhuman objects or events as created by human beings, i.e. that everything in the world was made by human beings for their use and enjoyment. For example, a child may believe that the sand was placed near the ocean for people to lie on, that a boulder was put in the backyard for children to jump from, etc.

Artificialism is similar to finalism; the child believes objects and events were created by a maker, either God or man. She may believe, for example, that God created rivers for people who wish to travel in boats.

Phenomenism refers to the notion that anything can be linked to anything else, although there is no real connection between them. Although the word "because" may be used, its true meaning is not understood. For example, a child may say that a boat floats because it is blue. Phenomenistic thinking is found primarily in very young children.

As the child grows older, precausal confusions are gradually replaced by causal thinking. However, vestiges of precausal thinking continue to exist well beyond childhood, and the question, "What has caused what?" is open to errors which are not confined to children alone. Many adults find it difficult to make causal judgments in particular cases. If event B follows event A, has A caused B? If it rains (event B) after an Indian dance (event A), has the dance caused the rain? Or could the two events be caused by a third event? Or are the rain and the dance unrelated events, even though their closeness in time or space suggests a real, not a coincidental relationship?

Our own notions of cause-and-effect are so well established that we cannot remember their absence in early childhood. We forget they were gradually acquired on the basis of different, sometimes erroneous, interpretations of observations and intuitive notions which helped us explain simple and recurring events.

* * *

Question: What is the child's concept of *dreams?* What is the influence of the precausal notion of *realism* on the child's thinking?

Instructions:

Ask the child each of the following questions, changing the

wording when necessary to include terms familiar to the child. (Be careful not to suggest more than is included in the instructions.)

I. General Questions

    A. Do you know what a dream is?

    B. Do you dream sometimes at night?

II. Specific Questions

    A. Origin of dreams

        1. Where does a dream come from?

        2. Are dreams made somewhere?

        3. Do they come from inside of you or from outside of you?

        4. Does somebody make the dreams come? (If child says yes, ask:)

            a. Is it you or someone else?

            b. Who?

    B. Location of dreams

        1. While you are dreaming, where is your dream?

        2. Is it inside of you, or in your room or where is it?

        3. (If the dream is *internal* — in the head, in the eyes, etc.)

            a. If we could look into your head while you are dreaming, could we see your dream?

            b. Why do you say that we could (not) see your dream?

        4. If the dream is *external* (in the room, on the walls, under the bed, close to the eyes, etc.)

            a. Is it in your room (on the wall, etc.) for real, or is it only as if it were there or make believe?

            b. While you are dreaming, are your eyes closed or open?

            c. When you dream that you are playing in the street, where is your dream? In the street, or in your room?

        5. In both cases

            a. Is there something in front of you while you are dreaming?

      b. Can your mother see your dream when she is in
         your room?
      c. If I were in your room, could I see your dream?
         Why?
  C. Organ of dreams
    1. What do we dream with?
    2. Is it with our hands?
    3. With what, then?
  D. Cause of dreams
    1. What did you dream about last?
    2. What made you dream about that?
       If the child says she did not dream say, "Let's make
       believe you dreamed you had fallen and hurt your-
       self . . ."
    3. Why would you dream about that?
    4. Do you know why we dream?
  E. Substance of dreams
    1. What is a dream made of?
    2. Is it made of paper?
    3. Then what is it made of?
    4. Can we touch our dreams?
    5. Why do you say that we can (cannot) touch our
       dreams?
  F. Reality of dreams
    1. During the night, when you dream you are playing, are
       you playing for real?
    2. Is it the same as when you are playing during the day?
    3. Can a dream come true?

Analysis

Stage I: four to five years

The child believes in the reality and tangibility of the dream,
and considers its origin external, e.g. "it came from the bed; the
window, etc." In her view, the dream does not depend on the
sleeper. There is little distinction at this level between subjective
and objective events.

Stage I Sample Responses

E: Do you know what a dream is?
C: It's people in the bed.
C: It comes in the window.

Origin of dreams:

C: In the bed; the dark; the window; the moon; in my heart.
C: Somebody else makes the dreams come.
C: It's Jesus in heaven.
C: If God wants us to see it we can see it.

Location of dreams:

C: It's in my bed; in my room; in the wall; just by our side; under my blanket.
C: No one can see it because it's in my pillow.
C: We dream with the face.
C: My mother turns the light on and the dream goes away.

Stage II: six to eight years

Transitional stage in regard to the distinction between objective events. The dream is believed to originate outside the child but goes on inside. The dream is accepted as a subjective event, but the child may believe that others can see the dream inside the head of the dreamer. Contradictions exist as to the origin, nature, and locale of the dream in relation to the dreamer.

Stage II Sample Responses

Origin of dreams:

C: It comes from the night when it's dark.

Location of dreams:

C: It's in my room.
C: It's inside of me sometimes.
C: You think about it and it falls into your head and it goes into your heart.
C: It's in our room, but we think about it with our head.
C: It's in front of me; by my side.
C: No one else can see it; it's invisible.

Stage III: eight years and up

The distinction between subjective and objective events is established, and the dream is viewed as an internal, personal, subjective event. The dream cannot be seen by others because, "it's my imagination, it's my thinking," etc.

Stage III Sample Responses

Origin of dreams:

C: *It's in the head; in the imagination; in the mind; in the eye.*
C: *It's from our thinking; our memory.*
C: *During the day you see something you don't like; then in the evening you dream, but you can dream a nice dream if you read a good book.*
C: *It comes from your subconscious.*

Location of dreams:

It's my imagination; we build it in ourselves; it's thinking and has no special place in your body.

* * *

Question: **What is the child's concept of *life?** What is the influence of the precausal notion of animism?**

  I. General Questions

      A. Do you know what it means to be alive, to be living?
      B. What does it mean?
      C. Give me the names of some things which are alive.

  II. Specific Questions – Individual Objects

      A. Is a mountain alive?
      B. Why do you say it is? (is not?)

---

*The definition of *life* according to Webster's New Twentieth Century Dictionary, Unabridged, Second Edition, 1970 is, "That property of plants and animals which makes it possible for them to take in food, get energy from it, grow, adapt themselves to their surroundings, and reproduce their kind; it is the quality that distinguishes a living animal or plant from inorganic matter or a dead organism."

C. Continue with the same format with the following.

the sun	an airplane
a table	a fire
an automobile	a fly
a cat	a flower
a cloud	the rain
a lamp	a tree
a watch	a snake
a bird	a bicycle
a bell	a fish
the wind	a pencil

Analysis

Stage I: under six years

Children attribute life to one or many inanimate objects (animistic thinking). They use criteria such as usefulness or movement, but their answers are frequently contradictory. Life is denied to plants.

Stage I Sample Responses

General Questions

C: It means we are alive and can do things.
C: It means you have a heart and blood.
C: It means you can run around.

Names of live things: cat, person, bird, turtle, wind.

Specific Questions

Mountain

C: Yes, it's alive; I saw fire coming out of it.
C: No, it doesn't have a mouth and a nose.

Sun

C: Yes, it gives light.
C: Yes, it moves around.

Table

C: No, it doesn't move.
C: Yes, because it stands up.

C: No, it doesn't have a heart and blood.
Cloud
C: Yes, it moves.
   Yes, it makes rain.

Stage II: seven to nine years

The child still resorts to criteria of Stage I but is now able to distinguish between objects which receive their impetus from an outside source and those which move by themselves. However, with unfamiliar and remote objects (clouds, sun, etc.) the child still tends to think animistically.

Stage II Sample Responses

General Questions
C: Alive means you're born.
   Alive means you can move; play; do things.
Names of live things: people, the sun.
Specific Questions
Mountain
C: No, it's not alive; it doesn't move; it can't eat.
Sun
C: Yes, it turns around.
   It's like us, it lies down and in the morning it wakes you up.
Table
C: No, because the tree it was made from is dead.
Cloud
C: Yes, because they bump together and the rain falls.

Stage III: ten years and up

Disappearance of animistic thinking. The concept of life is applied only to humans and animals. Occasionally life is still refused to plants.

Stage III Sample Responses,

General Questions
C: We're not dead, our blood keeps running.
Names of live things: person, animals, vegetables, fruit.
Specific Questions

Mountain

C: No, it's not like a human being; it can't grow or eat.

Sun

C: No, it's like a light; it's inorganic.

Table

C: No, it's made of wood, which was once alive.

C: No, it can't replace itself.

Cloud

C: No, it's water vapor.

C: No, it's not an animal or a person; it doesn't speak or breathe.

C: No, it doesn't replace itself,

* * *

Question: Does the child understand the *causes of the floating and sinking of objects?* What is the influence of precausal notions?

The following summarizes some physics concepts essential to an understanding of floating and sinking.

1. *Density:* This refers to the relationship of mass to volume. For example, the density of a piece of copper is found by dividing the mass of any piece of copper by its volume. A "heavy" object has a high density and a "light" object has low density.

2. The density of various materials is compared by means of their *specific gravity.* The specific gravity of a substance is the relationship of its density to that of water. That is, if the density of an object is higher than that of water, i.e. if it is "heavier" than water, it sinks, if lighter, it floats.

   The specific gravity of a substance is expressed in relationship to the specific gravity of water. The specific gravity of water is arbitrarily set at 1.0. For example, a substance with a density two times that of water has a specific gravity of 2.0. If the density of another material is half that of water, it is 0.5, etc. For example, the specific gravity of white pine is .35, which explains its floating, while that for platinum is 21.4, which explains its sinking.

3. Why does a 30,000 ton ocean liner made largely of metal float? This is explained by the *law of flotation* which states

that a floating body displaces a weight of liquid equal to its own weight.

A change of shape redistributes weight. Why does a 30,000 ton ship float and a 30,000 ton nail sink; Because of their difference in shape, their density differs despite the fact that their mass is the same. The nail is too dense to float, i.e. it does not displace enough water to be buoyed up. Archimedes' principle states that a body immersed in water is buoyed up by a force equal to the weight of the water displaced. The ship will float because its weight is distributed over a larger area. That is, it is less dense and therefore able to displace more water than did the nail.

Materials: 1 rectangular plastic container (about 6″ x 4″ x 4″or larger)
2 cylindrical plastic containers (about 2″ x 1″)
1 plasticine ball about 1½″ in diameter
5 objects: a small boat, a glass marble, a wooden bead, a nail, a wooden peg

Instructions:

Fill the large container about three quarters full of water and place it in front of child.

Part I: Floating and sinking of varied objects

Present the following items successively. Allow the child to feel the weight of each item if she so desires. Let her place the objects in the water herself to increase interest.

E: (Show the boat.) *If we put this boat in the water, will it float or will it sink to the bottom?*

E: Why do you think it will . . . (float or sink, depending on child's response)?

(If child predicted it would sink.)

E: Why does it stay on top of the water, why doesn't it go to the bottom?

E: (Show the marble.) *If we put this marble in the water, will it float or will it sink to the bottom?*

E: Why do you think it will . . . (float or sink, depending on child's response)?

If child predicted it would float, drop the marble in the water.

E: Why does it sink?

Show the wooden bead and proceed exactly as in A.
Show the nail and proceed exactly as in B.
Show the wooden peg and proceed exactly as in A.

In all the preceding problems, as well as in the following, if the child just explains the floating or sinking by the substance the object is made of (because it's made of wood, because it's made of glass, etc.) ask her each time to explain further, say, for instance:

E: *Why does it float when it's made of wood?*

Part II: Floating and sinking of objects of similar appearance

Nail and Wooden Peg

Take all the objects, except the nail and the wooden peg out of the water.

E: *See, only the nail and the peg are left. Why did the nail sink to the bottom and the peg float to the top?*

Take the nail and the peg out. Take the marble and the wooden bead and put them (or have child put them) in the water.

E: *Watch again. The marble sank to the bottom and the bead floated on top, Why? Can you explain it to me?*

Take out the marble and bead.

Part III: Sinking of a small object in comparison
              with the floating of a large object

E: *Have you ever seen a large boat? Tell me why large boats float on top of the water?*

If the explanation is based on the movement of the boats, (they move, they have a motor, sails, oars, etc.) ask again, before going on.

E: *If the large boats didn't move, if they were standing still* (if they didn't have a motor, oars, etc.) *would they sink?*

E: *Explain why they . . .* (float or sink, depending on child's response).

E: *Which is heavier, a large boat or a small marble like this one?*
   (hand the child the marble.)
   Does the marble sink to the bottom?
   Does a large boat stay on top of the water?
   Why does a large boat float on top of the water and a marble sink to the bottom?

Which is heavier, if you hold them, the large boat or the small marble?
Why does the boat float on the water?
In a large lake, would the marble still sink to the bottom?

Part IV: Floating and sinking of plasticine

Remove all objects from the large container. Show the child the plasticine ball (she may weigh it if she wishes).

E: If I put this in the water, will it float on the water or will it sink to the bottom?
Explain why you think it will . . . (float or sink, depending on child's response).

Put the ball in the water. If the child's prediction was correct, make her realize she was right. If her prediction was wrong, ask her to explain why the plasticine ball went down to the bottom. Then take the ball out, give it to the child.

E: Try to fix it so that it will stay on top of the water, so that it will float. Make something with the plasticine. Can you do something to it so that it will float, so that it will not sink to the bottom? What do you think you have to do to it to make it float?

Let the child work and record exactly what she does (whether she tries to make smaller and smaller balls, whether she tries to make the ball hollow, to form some kind of boat, etc.) When the child wants to test her answer by putting her construction in the water, let her do so, but make a note of it. If the child then realizes she did not succeed in making it float and wants to try again, let her keep on trying with as many trials as she wishes during a maximum five-minute time period. However, make detailed notes of each one of these trials. During these various attempts, try to make the child give, if she does not do so spontaneously, the reasons for the different transformations of the plasticine ball. If the child succeeds in making the plasticine float, ask her the following sequence of questions.

E: Why does it float now when it's like this?
What makes it float?
Why did the ball sink to the bottom a moment ago, and now float on the water?

If the child does not succeed in making the plasticine float, model it into a boat shape. Set it in the water.

E: You see, it floats now. Why do you think it floats now that I've changed its shape? What makes it float now? Why did the ball sink to the bottom and this shape float?

Analysis

Stage I: four to six years

Explanations at this stage are precausal, mainly finalistic (the boat floats because it's made to float), animistic (it's afraid to sink), or artificialistic (the government makes boats float).

Stage I Sample Responses

Boats

C: If it didn't float, people would drown.
If you would wait, it would go to the bottom.
It doesn't want to drop.

Marble

C: It will sink because it's a ball.
It will sink because the boat is there.
It sinks because it's blue.
It will sink because it's not supposed to be in the water.

Nail and Peg

C: There's a man in the stick and he's mad. He doesn't want to let himself go to the bottom and the man in the nail lets himself go to the bottom.

Plasticine

Rarely solved at this level. Child either refuses to do anything with it or molds it into various shapes without hollowing it out.

Stage II: seven to nine years

Child offers a physical explanation, but with contradictions and misconceptions. She may use volume, weight, substance, shape, or quantity of the water, but precausal beliefs such as dynamism persist.

Stage II Sample Responses

Boat

C: It will sink because it's small.
It will sink because it's heavy and can go down.

It will float because it's wood.
It will float because there's a lot of water.
Everything heavy floats and everything light sinks.

Marble

C: *It will sink because it's heavier.*
It goes down because it's small.
It sinks because there's air inside.
The marble isn't heavy, but the boat is big.

Plasticine

Floating is connected with lightness and children try to make small pieces. They tend to make them "thin" because "it is less heavy like that."

Stage III: ten to twelve years

Boat

C: *A boat floats because it's built like this* (gestures).
The boat displaces a lot of water but the marble doesn't displace enough water for its weight.
The marble is small and it weighs a lot. The boat weighs less for its size.

Plasticine

Child can explain that:

1. The change in shape produced a larger displacement of water which was then sufficient to hold the plasticine, and
2. The transformation of the shape of the plasticine modifies its density and therefore its weight.

JUDGMENT AND REASONING

Use of Causal Conjunctions

Piaget believes that children often think and act logically before they can express logic in their language. In his early work, he studied children's use of words expressing logical relationships. His research showed that although a child may use words (such as the conjunction "because") correctly in a grammatical sense, he does not necessarily use words correctly in a logical sense. In general, the young child who does not understand cause-and-effect relationships is unable to express such relationships in words.

Thus, in constructing sentences, the four-year-old child may simply state that two events, A and B, occurred. He does not yet know that one event, A, may have *caused* the other event, B, to occur. A four-year-old may construct the following sentence: The man broke his leg, *and* he fell off his bike. He merely states that the two events occurred, not that one event has caused the other. The seven or eight-year-old child, on the other hand, may construct the following sentence: The man broke his leg *because* he fell off his bike. He now understands a causal relationship and can express it in language: A has caused B.

The younger child does not differentiate between cause-and-effect relationships and sequences of events, and thus cannot assign specific words to these relationships. He senses a relationship, but cannot express it clearly. As a result, he may use conjunctions such as "because," "but," and "so," but they do not necessarily signify logical relationships. The conjunctions are used simply to tie together two statements, as the word "and" might be used. Questioning frequently reveals that although the child uses words expressing causal relationships, he does not necessarily understand them.

Understanding Reciprocal Relationships

Child: Mommy, why doesn't Grandma have any children?
Mother: I'm Grandma's child. She's my mother.
Child: But you're a mommy; you can't be a child.

Piaget investigated children's understanding of the logical concept of class by questioning their understanding of family relationships. For example, in order for a child to understand his relationship to his mother, he must coordinate (1) the idea that she is a member of the class of mothers with (2) another idea, that of his relationship to her as child. A young child may define the concept "mother" simply as "a woman," thus using only the idea of class and not of relationship. For example, the child who has acquired the word "mommy" knows that the word refers to *his* mommy, and now applies the word to all women. This is an overgeneralization which occurs because the concept "mommy" is only partially comprehended and defined. To the young child it means only that "mommy" is a member of the class of women. The other part of the definition, which places "mommy" in a particular relationship to the child himself, is omitted. The child cannot perceive the relationship because, egocentrically, he views the relationship only from his own perspective. In order to understand his relationship to his mother, he would also have to understand the relationship of his mother to his father and to other siblings. Egocentrism prevents him from perceiving his mother's relationship to other people. In addition to the limitations of egocentrism, he is unable to deal with two aspects of a situation at the same time.

Difficulty in grasping two-way relationships may be noted in the child's understanding of brother/sister relationships. Young children find it difficult to see themselves as brothers and sisters of their own siblings. For the young child, "Howard is my brother," does not necessarily imply "I am Howard's brother." This relationship is not usually clarified until the age of nine or ten. The relational concepts of left and right, which also depend upon awareness of several points of view at the same time are not understood until the ages of eleven or twelve.

* * *

Question: Does the child *use causal conjunctions to express logical connections?* Are the conjunctions *"because," "but," "although,"* used to explain relationships?

Instructions:

Ask the child to complete the following:
1. I won't go to school tomorrow, because . . .
2. That man fell off his bicycle because . . .
3. Paul says he saw a little cat swallow a big dog. That's not possible because . . .
4. I read the book, because . . .
5. He ate the ice cream, but . . .
6. Ernest is playing in the street, even though . . .
7. He slapped my face even though . . .
8. I ate another apple, even though . . .
9. She saw the movie, but . . .
10. It is hot today, although . . .
11. He had a bath yesterday, although . . .
12. I didn't get wet yesterday, although . . .
13. Jake lost his pen, but . . .

Analysis

Stage I: under six years

Connectives are not used with logical meaning. "And" and "because" are interchangeable and other conjunctions are rarely used. The child's language does not express causal relations or sequential events.

Stage I Sample Responses

C: That man fell off his bicycle because he's not riding.
C: I didn't get wet yesterday and I had an umbrella.
C: I ate another apple and I was hungry.
C: That man fell off his bicycle because he hurt himself.

Stage II: seven to nine years

Transitional stage in which confusion between the various possible relations is shown. Some conjunctions *(and,* sometimes *because)* are appropriately used; however, conjunctions expressing exception (but, although, even though) are not comprehended.

Stage II Sample Responses

C: That man fell off his bicycle because he broke his arm.
C: He had a bath yesterday although afterwards he was clean.
C: I won't go to school tomorrow because I am sick.

Stage III: over ten years

Child can handle words expressing causal relationships and sequential events implied in "because" as well as the exceptions implied in "but," "although," and "even though."

Stage III Sample Responses

C: I didn't get wet yesterday, although it rained all day.
C: Ernest is playing in the street, even though it's dangerous.
C: Jake lost his pen, but he borrowed one for the test.

* * *

Question: Is the child able to understand family relationships such as *brother-sister relationships?*

Instructions:

Ask the child the following questions (If the child has no brothers and sisters omit questions 1, 2 and 3, start with 4.):

1. *E: How many brothers do you have? How many sisters?* (If

child has brother A and sister B): *And how many*
brothers does B have? And how many sisters? And how
many brothers does A have? And how many sisters?

2. *E: How many brothers are there in the family? How many*
sisters? How many brothers and sisters altogether?

3. *E: Are you a brother* (or sister)? *What is a brother* (or
sister?

4. *E: There are three brothers in a family, Michael, David and*
Andrew. How many brothers does Michael have? And
David? And Andrew?

5. *E: Barbara has three sisters, Susan, Ellen, and Debbie. How*
many sisters does Susan have? And Ellen? And Debbie?
How many sisters are there in this family?

Analysis

Stage I: under five years

Children find it difficult to see themselves as brothers or sisters
of their own siblings and may not include themselves in the total
number of brothers and sisters. They consider brothers and sisters
from their own points of view, counting them without including
themselves, or counting the family as a whole. They simply define
brother as "a boy," sister as "a girl."

Stage I Sample Responses

E: *Have you got a sister?*
C: *Yes.*
E: *And has she got a sister?*
C: *No, she hasn't got a sister. I am my sister.*
E: *Have you any brothers?*
C: *Gerry.*
E: *And has Gerry got a brother?*
C: *No, only me has a brother.*
E: *Are you sure Gerry doesn't have a brother?*
C: *No, he don't.*

Stage II: six to seven years

The child understands that there must be two or more children
in the family in order to call one a brother or sister, but the
concept is not truly relational. He doesn't count himself among

the brothers and sisters; they're a separate group. Later he begins
to realize he should include himself.

Stage II Sample Responses

Child 1

E: *Have you any brothers?*
C: *Two, Paul and Martin.*
E: *Does Paul have any brothers?*
C: *No.*
E: *Aren't you his brother?*
C: *Yes.*
E: *Then does Paul have any brothers?*
C: *No.*

Child 2

E: *Do you have any sisters?*
C: *Ethel.*
E: *Does she have a sister?*
C: *No.*
E: *How many sisters are there in the family?*
C: *Two.*
E: *Do you have any?*
C: *One.*
E: *Does Ethel have any?*
C: *None at all.*
E: *Are you her sister?*
C: *Yes.*
E: *Then she does have a sister?*
C: *No.*

Child 3

E: *Do you have a brother?*
C: *Yes.*
E: *Does your brother have a brother?*
C: *No.*
E: *Are you sure?*
C: *Yes.*
E: *Does your sister have a brother?*
C: *No.*

E: Is your brother also your sister's brother?
C: No.
E: Does your brother have a sister?
C: No.
E: How many brothers are there in your family?
C: One.
E: Then you're not a brother?
C: Yes.
E: Then your brother has a brother?
C: Yes.
E: How many?
C: One.
E: Who is it?
C: Me.

Stage III: over nine years

The child understands the brother/sister relationship. The point of view of relation and the point of view of membership are clearly distinguished.

Stage III Sample Responses

C: A brother is when there are two boys in the family and they are related. They have the same parents.

* * *

Question: Does the child have a concept of *the relationship of left to right?*

Materials: Coin, pencil, key, bracelet

Instructions:

E: Show me your right hand. Now your left. Show me your right leg. Now your left. (Note: Discontinue if child cannot respond correctly.)
E: (While sitting opposite child) *Show me my right hand. Now my left. Show me my right leg. Now my left.*
E: (Place coin on table to the left of a pencil in relation to the child.) *Is the pencil to the right or to the left? And the penny?*

E: (Child is opposite experimenter, who has a coin in one hand and a bracelet on the left arm.) *You see this penny? Have I got it in my right hand or in my left? And the bracelet?*

E: (Child is opposite three objects in a row: a pencil to the left, a key in the middle, and coin to the right.) *Is the pencil to the left or to the right of the key? And of the penny? And of the pencil? Is the penny to the left or the right of the pencil? And of the key?*

E: (The same questions with three objects in a row opposite the child; a key to the left, a piece of paper in the middle, and a pencil to the right. The objects are only shown for half a minute and are then covered.) *I'm going to show you three things for a moment. Look at them very carefully. Then I'll cover them and ask you to tell me how they were arranged. Look* (time elapses). *Now, was the key left or right of the piece of paper, and of the pencil* (etc.)?

Analysis

Stage I: under six years

The child can correctly identify his own right and left hands and legs, but not those of the experimenter facing him. Right and left are considered only from his own point of view.

Stage II: seven to eleven years

Right and left are also considered from the point of view of the person who is speaking to him, but not in terms of the things. When three objects are placed in a row in front of him, a pencil, a key, and a coin, he can say that the pencil is on the left and the coin is on the right, and the key is in the middle. He usually does not grasp that the key is simultaneously to the right of the pencil and to the left of the coin.

Stage III: over eleven years

Right and left are also considered in relation to the things themselves and are seen as relative rather than fixed.

SPACE

This story of a three-year-old child illustrates how concepts of space grow out of motor acts:

> While visiting a department store, a child was taken up a flight of stairs and down by a different flight. The next day, on visiting the store again, she was taken up the stairs she had come down previously. The child protested that these were the 'going down' stairs and the others were the 'going up' stairs.

According to Piaget, the child gradually develops and coordinates her ideas about space as she develops her other notions about the world. That is, she learns from actual manipulation of objects, not merely by passive observation. In infancy, space is probably no more than concrete "spaces" surrounding given objects. Slowly, in the course of development, the many "spaces" are constructed into an abstract idea: one space.

Developmental Stages

By about four months of age the rapid maturation of the nervous system enables the infant to coordinate the movements of her eyes and hands. As she discovers and observes the movement of her hand in space, she establishes for herself an idea of the space surrounding her hand. She also becomes aware of other spaces as well: the space between her body and the body of the caretaking adult, the space between her body and the side of the crib, between her hand and a toy, etc. Space to the young child is still subjective and temporary. She is the measure of all things; she learns about space in relation to herself only, with herself as the central and only important factor in the universe. She is unable to view herself, as adults do, as merely another element in an all-encompassing space.

The acquisition of language does not change the toddler's spatial egocentrism. To a stranger's question about where she lives, she may reply that she lives in a red house with a black door, assuming that everyone knows what she knows and that everyone can find her house because she can. She is unaware of the existence of, or need for, objective systems for locating points in space, such as the directions north or south, the expression of distances in miles, angles, degrees, or even a street address with a number. She is still unable to describe the world using an objective reference system. During the school years, she gradually acquires concepts of perspective, angularity, parallelism, and distance.

How do concepts of space develop? By the time a child is four, she can make certain spatial discriminations. For example, she can distinguish objects on the basis of certain criteria referred to as *topological;* she can distinguish open from closed, an object with a hole from one without a hole, a closed loop with something inside from a loop with something outside, etc. The concept of topological space is followed by the development of concepts of a *projective* character, where objects are viewed, not in isolation, but with regard to other objects. This is followed by concepts of *Euclidean* space, which deals with geometrical figures, angles, etc. The child's ability to draw and distinguish curved figures (topological space) is mastered before she attains the ability to project her angle of vision along a line (projective space) and to draw and distinguish figures with angles (Euclidean space).

* * *

Question: Does the child have the ability to draw shapes with **(A) topological** and **(B) Euclidean properties.***

Materials: 21 shapes to be copied as shown in the following diagram. Some emphasize topological relationships, some simple Euclidean shapes.

---

*Topological deals with open and closed figures such as a simple closed curve. Euclidean deals with angularity, parallelism, and distance.

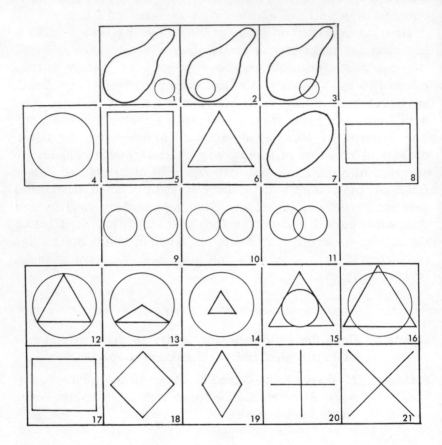

Analysis

Stage I: up to four years

Open shapes are distinguished from closed ones; circle is drawn as an irregular closed curve. Squares and triangles are not distinguished from circles.

Stage I Responses

Eric 3;8

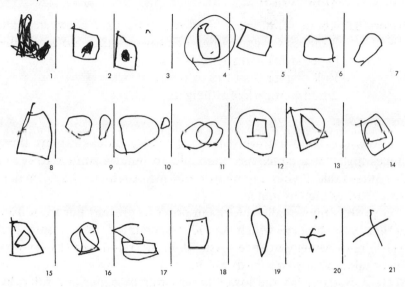

Stage II: five to seven years

Curved shapes begin to be distinguished from straight-sided ones, but the latter remain undifferentiated. Shapes begin to be gradually distinguished according to their angles. Square is separated from triangle, as is circle from ellipse. Numbers 17 and 19 are successfully reproduced, but not number 18. The rhombus is drawn correctly and circumscribed figures gradually mastered.

Stage III: from seven years up

All problems overcome, including composite figures.

* * *

Question: Does the child *use measuring instruments spontaneously* in a task which cannot be adequately mastered without them?

Materials: About 40 blocks: 12 of the same size, between 2 and 3 inches, for experimenter's tower, other blocks smaller
Paper strips and sticks
Ruler larger than the tower
2 tables of different heights

Instructions:

Show the child a tower made of twelve blocks, about thirty inches high, on a table. Ask the child to build a similar tower on the other table. Avoid any mention of measurement. Say, "make a tower just as high as mine."

Give the child smaller blocks in order to prevent her from using similar size blocks which could be counted and result in a one-to-one correspondence. Ask child to build her tower on a lower table, about two yards away.

Have available on the lower table strips of paper and ruler, but do not mention using them as measures. When her spontaneous efforts have been exhausted, tell her to use the paper strips or ruler in order to measure the experimenter's tower.

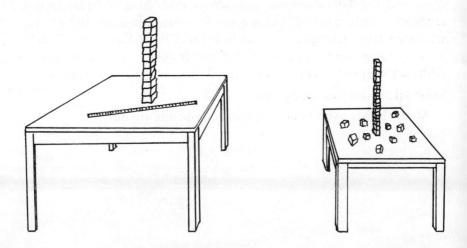

Analysis

Stage I: four to five years

Visual comparison is the only basis of comparison between the model and the copy. There is no measurement, and no measuring instruments are used.

Stage I Sample Responses

E: Is your tower just as high as mine? Did you measure it?
C: Oh yes, just look at it.
   By looking at the blocks you can see.
   They're the same height; I got good eyes.

Stage II: five to seven years

Objects are moved in the process of measurement. For example, the child brings the experimenter's tower closer to the child's table. The comparison, however, is still visual. Appraisal is more efficient; the child may begin to use her own body to measure. The span of hands or arms is sometimes used to transfer a distance from the model to the copy.

Stage II Sample Responses

E: Is your tower as high as mine? How would you measure it?
C: Put a stick across from there to there (joins tower tops).
   Put the new tower up against the old one.
   I could use my arm or my fingers.
   You could mark this piece of paper (held vertically).

Stage III: seven to eight years

The child's body as a measurement is replaced by another object having the same height as the tower. In the early part of Stage III, it does not occur to the child to mark off the length she wants. Gradually measurement is used. The child then can use a large ruler to mark off the required length and to remember it while transferring it to the copy.

Stage III Sample Responses

E: How would you measure?
C: You could take a ruler and measure them.
   You have to mark off the length.
   You have to take their measurements (using large ruler).

* * *

Question: Does the child comprehend the *concept of projective constructions?*
How does the child construct a straight line?

Materials: Large rectangular table
10 colored plastic toothpicks or matchsticks on plasticene bases

Instructions:

> *These are telephone poles,* (indicate toothpicks on bases), *and I would like you to set them up so they will be in a straight line beside a straight road. I will put in the one that will be in the beginning of the line and the one that will be at the end of the line. I would like you to put in the ones in between that make the straight line.*

Part 1: Place the toothpicks parallel to the edge of the table.
Part 2: Put the toothpicks at an angle to the table.

Analysis

Stage I: up to four years

Child cannot form a straight line even when it runs parallel to the table.

Stage I Sample Responses

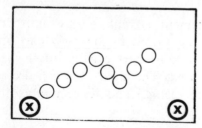
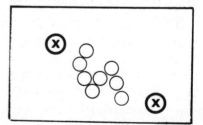

Stage II: four to seven years

During the early stage the child uses a topological approach; that is, she sets each post next to the preceding one on the basis of proximity rather than the projection of a straight line. The child can form a straight line when it runs parallel to the table, but not when it is at an angle.

Stage II Sample Responses

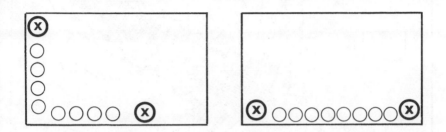

Stage III: seven years and up

Child can construct a straight line no matter where it lies on the table. Child spontaneously aims or sights along the path, putting herself in line with the two posts to be linked by the straight line.

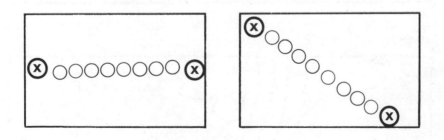

* * *

Question: Can the child learn to *locate the position of an object (a) in a structured framework, (b) in a rotated structured framework?*

Materials: 2 boards, approximately 15 x 20 inches
10 blocks to represent houses (2 identical series of 5) consisting of 1 red, 1 yellow, 3 other colors
2 little toy figures

Instructions:

Part I: Draw roads and railroad tracks on two boards as

indicated in diagram. Place the two landscape boards on the table
in front of the child so they face the same direction for the child.

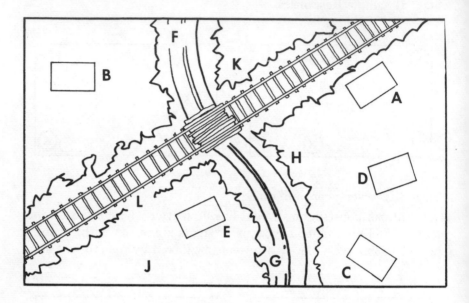

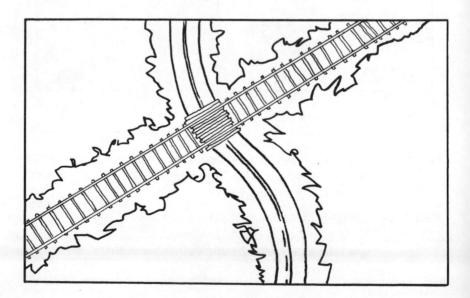

E: We're going to play a game. We have two pictures that are alike. Here is a road for cars, and on the other picture there's a road just like it. Here is a railroad track for trains, and on the other picture there's one just like it. You see the two pictures are exactly alike. Now I'll take this picture (Board A) *and have you take one* (Board B).

E: Now we're going to put houses on our pictures. We'll put the houses in the same place on both the pictures. See, here I'm putting a red house on my picture. You put a red house on your picture. Put one in the same place so the two pictures will be exactly alike. (Place houses as indicated in A, B, C, D, E.)

E: Now the two pictures are still exactly alike. You have houses just like mine and they're in the same place.

E: I have a little person, and I'm giving you one just like mine. I'm going to put my person in my picture. Then you put your person in the same place in your picture. You put your person just the way mine is (Position F).

Allow child to place figure. If she does not understand the instructions, place it for her explaining again. Then present the person, repeating the same procedure, in position G. Once the instructions are understood, place figures in positions H, J, K, L, each time asking the child to locate her figure in the same way.

Part II: Remove the two figures, leave houses arranged in the same way. Rotate board A one half-turn, or 180 degrees.

E: I'm turning my picture. You see it's still just like yours, but it's turned. I still have a road (point), *railroad tracks, a red house* (enumerate and point). *Now I'm going to put my person in the picture again. You put yours in the same place as mine, just like mine, at the same place in your picture. I'm putting my person on the red house. Put yours in the same place, in the same position in your picture.*

Repeat instructions if necessary using yellow house. Then place figures in same successive positions as in Part I, each time asking child to place her figure in the same place.

Analysis

Stage I: under five years

Solutions are egocentric. Strategies used are confined to

relationships such as neighborhood, enclosure, and symmetry, which are too elementary for accuracy. The child cannot estimate distances and coordinate relationships. She uses cues such as "beside the house," "on the road," etc.

Stage I Sample Responses

Part I: Child solves A and B. C produces a symmetrical response (opposite first house). F is solved without hesitation. In H she places person against the red house rather than between the house and road. She misses D, E, J, K.

Stage II: six to seven years

Part I: Begins to recognize projective dimensions and to coordinate them, but remains basically egocentric. Gradual success with first part of test, since she is now able to establish directional relations with respect to her own body. Notions of laterality and depth are gradually substituted for symmetry and gesture imitation. Child establishes a fixed reference point.

Part II: Child is only able to place figure in positions corresponding to her own perspective; she is unable to reverse the left-right and before-behind dimensions.

Stage II Sample Responses

Part I: All problems solved.

Part II: In A, person is placed between red house and railroad tracks (egocentric response) then moved to correct position. Same treatment in B. Responses to C and D determined by neighborhood: person is placed between the two houses facing the red house. E is solved after correcting an initial egocentric response. F is not solved; G solved immediately. H, the person is too close to the house. I and J missed; unable to coordinate the two necessary dimensions. In K, symmetry prevails; she places person between road and house. In L, she cannot give up her own point of view.

Stage III: eight years and up

Child is gradually able to abandon egocentric perspective and reverse the left-right and before-behind relationships. She is capable of the necessary coordinations and reversals, although sometimes laboriously. Trial and error gradually become systematic analysis.

Stage III Sample Responses

Part I: Complete success.

Part II: A through G solved with no hesitation, except G where figure is placed first on road and then brought back to position. H and I immediately solved. Hesitates on J, then places correctly. L is placed near intersection of road and railroad tracks, but in the sector containing the yellow house (correct in relation, but incorrect in relation to tracks).

TIME, MOVEMENT, AND SPEED

What is the meaning of the statement, the car traveled at a speed of sixty miles per hour? What does it tell us about the relationships of time, distance, and speed? While we, as adults, are aware of the logical connections among these three concepts, do we expect children to acquire all at the same time? Or does each concept undergo a separate development? Does the acquisition of one concept depend upon the acquisition of the other two?

Although the three concepts, time, distance, and speed, are related logically, children do not comprehend them as related until their thinking has developed to the level of the late concrete operational or early formal operational period. The fact that the child appears to be unable to relate the three concepts logically prevents him also, of course, from comprehending each one separately. Despite the fact that each task can only be understood with reference to the other two, we shall outline the development of each concept separately. For example, we shall explore the development of the notions of time and of distance, on which an understanding of speed depends. That is, when we say that the car traveled at a speed of sixty miles per hour, we define speed as the relationship between time, or duration (1 hour), and distance (60 miles).

Time and Age Concepts

David Elkind relates that on the evening of his birthday, his four-year-old son announced, "Daddy, you don't need any more birthdays; you're all grown up already." (N. Y. Times, Oct. 11, 1970)

Early in life the child forms intuitive notions about time. The infant waiting to be fed or picked up probably experiences the passage of time. He gradually learns that certain events, such as mealtimes, follow each other in order, and thus he develops a concept of "before" and "after," a concept of sequence or succession. As he learns the order of events through constant repetition, he becomes aware of time intervals between them. In this way he develops an intuitive understanding of time based on the succession of events and the duration of intervals. According to Piaget, an adequate concept of time requires the coordination of both the succession of events and the duration of intervals.

The very young child probably cannot conceive of the abstract idea of "time," but rather considers time to be a concrete and localized series of "times," such as nap time, meal time, etc. From these individual instances of time, the child must abstract the idea of one "time" to understand the meaning of the abstraction "time." He must not only coordinate the succession of events with the duration of intervals, but he must also become aware of time relative to the present time; that tomorrow will become today which, in turn, will become yesterday.

In the toddler, notions such as tomorrow, or next week, if they assume meaning at all, probably communicate no more than waiting. For example, "we cannot go to the beach until tomorrow," means simply, "another time" or "not now." Similarly, a concept such as "last week" or "last year" or even "yesterday" simply means "not at this time" or maybe "never again." Past events appear to be less important to the child. Memory functions for short time periods only; past events have little meaning and are not remembered. It is therefore not surprising that vocabulary studies show the word "today" to be acquired by twenty-four months, the word "tomorrow" by thirty months, while the word "yesterday" is not acquired until thirty-six months of age. Despite the fact that these words exist by thirty-six months, their use relative to the present time (tomorrow will be today, today will be yesterday) will not be understood until many years later.

We shall use the concept of age to illustrate one aspect of children's difficulties with time. The following confusions are often found in the three to six-year-old group in regard to age.

Children confuse size with age and consider the taller person the older person.

Children do not realize that age differences, i.e. succession, are fixed and preserved throughout life. A child may believe that if he is older than his brother this year, to be fair, the brother will have a chance to be older than he is next year.

Similarly, children believe that the duration of intervals, e.g. years, are not constant. They think that as they grow older and bigger, they will catch up with their parents in age. They become confused by observing size differences, which indeed even out when full size is attained.

The child's idea of time is static and discontinuous. The passage of time is not experienced as a flow, but as a series of static events. For example, one is four and one-half years old until a birthday suddenly propels one into being five years old.

There follows an intermediate or transitional stage, at six or seven years, during which the child understands notions of succession and duration and can use one but not both simultaneously; that is, he cannot integrate them. Finally, at about the age of seven or eight, he is able to coordinate succession and duration and construct for himself reasonable ideas of age and time.

* * *

Question: How does the child's *notion of age* develop?

Instructions:

Ask the child the following questions:
1. Do you have a brother?
   Do you have a sister?
   (if neither) Do you have a friend?
2. How old is your brother? Or sister? Or friend?
3. Who is older, you or your brother, (sister, or friend)?
4. Who will be older next year?
5. Who will be older when you are grown up?
6. Who was born first, you or your brother, (sister, or friend)?
7. Is your mother older than you?
   Is your father older than you?
8. Does your father (mother) get older every year?
9. Do you get older every year?

10. How much longer will you keep on getting older?
11. Who was born first, your mother or you?
12. What makes you get older?
13. How old can anybody get?
14. When people are grown up, can they get older?
15. Who is older, your father or your mother?
16. Who was born first, your father or your mother?
17. Are you getting older as quickly as your brother (or your sister, or your friend)?
18. What happens to your age when you have a birthday?
19. How many birthdays can you have in one year?
20. When you are an old man (or an old woman), will you still be the same number of years older or younger than your brother, (your sister, or your friend)?
21. When you are old, will you still have birthdays?

Analysis

Stage I: under six years

Child does not relate age to the number of years elapsed since birth. Age is confused with height; the taller is believed to be the older. Aging is not understood to be a continuous process, but is related to a given point in time, such as a birthday. A child believes he is four until the day of his birthday, when he becomes five. Age differences are not maintained throughout life. For example, one year he can be older than his sister and next year the order can be reversed.

Stage I Sample Responses

E: How old is Erica? (sister)
C: Don't know.
E: Is she a baby?
C: No, she can walk.
E: Who is older?
C: Me.
E: Why?
C: Because I'm the bigger one.
E: Who will be older when she starts going to school?
C: I don't know.

E: Is your mother older than you?
C: Yes.
E: Is your grandmother older than your mother?
C: No, she's young.
E: Is your grandfather older than your father?
C: They're the same age; they're as big as each other.
E: Will you be the same age next year?
C: No, I'll have my birthday.

Stage II: seven to eight years

The child believes either that (1) age depends on the order of births, but age differences are not maintained throughout life, or (2) that age differences are maintained but do not depend on the order of births.

Stage II Sample Responses

Child 1

E: Are you the same age as your sister?
C: No, because we weren't born at the same time.
E: Who was born first?
C: She was.
E: Will you be the same age as she one day?
C: Soon I'll be bigger than her because men are bigger than women. Then I'll be older.
E: Who is older, you or your brother?
C: I am.
E: Who was born first?
C: I was.
E: When you're grown up what age will your brother be?
C: The same as me.

Child 2

E: Is your friend older than you?
C: Yes, five years older.
E: Was he born before or after you?
C: He didn't tell me.
E: Are you getting old as quickly as each other?
C: Yes.
E: When you're very old will there be the same difference?
C: Yes.

Stage III: nine years

The child understands that age depends on the order of births, on years elapsed since birth, and that age differences are maintained throughout life.

Stage III Sample Responses

Child 1

E: Is your friend older or younger than you?

C: He's the same age. He was born in the same year so he must be the same age.

Child 2

C: I have two brothers, Jim and Scott.

E: Who was born first?

C: First me, then Jim, then Scott.

E: When you are grown up how old will you all be?

C: I'll be the oldest, then Jim, then Scott.

E: Why?

C: It's always the same. It all depends on when you were born.

* * *

Questions: Does the child understand the *relationship between size and age?*

Materials: Pictures of twins at five different time periods, with one member of the set growing taller than the other one.

Instructions:

E: Here is a set of twins, a boy and a girl. Do you know what twins are? Look at these pictures of them growing up.

Picture 1. *In this picture, is one of the twins older than the other one? Which one? Why?*

Picture 2. *In this picture, are both twins older than in the first picture?*

Picture 2. *In this picture, is one of the twins older than the other one? Which one? Why?*

Picture 3. *In this picture, is one of the twins older than the other one? Which one? Why?*

Picture 4. *In this picture, is one of the twins older than the other one? Which one? Why?*

Picture 5. *Are the twins ever the same age as each other? Why?*

Analysis

Stage I: under six years

Age is confused with height; the taller is believed to be the older. Age differences are not maintained throughout life; one year a child can be older than his twin and younger the next.

Stage I Sample Responses

C: The boy is older; he's bigger.
C: She's taller than him now. She's older.
C: They're the same age because they're the same size.

Stage II: seven to eight years

The child is puzzled when size differences are present in persons of the same age.

Stage II Sample Responses

C: I think they're the same age.
It's funny; he looks bigger.

Stage III: over nine years

The child understands that age depends on years elapsed since birth and that age and size are not perfectly correlated.

Stage III Sample Responses

C: They're the same age because they were born at the same time.
C: It doesn't matter that he's taller than she is.

* * *

Question: Does the child understand the *concept of time as related to distance traveled?*

Materials: 2 dolls

Instructions:

Hold one doll in each hand. Tell child to say "go" and after a short while to say "stop." Start dolls at same point and same time when child says "go." Make each doll hop along; however, make one doll take longer hops than the other. When child says "stop," one doll should be further along than the other.

E: Did both dolls start at the same time?
 Did both dolls stop at the same time?
 Did one doll go as far as the other doll?
 Did they both hop for the same length of time?

If the answer to the second question is "no," ask the following.

E: When one stopped was the other one still going?

Analysis

Stage I: under five years

The child bases judgment of time on how much ground has been covered or how fast an action has taken place, without relating the two.

Stage I Sample Responses

C: They started when I said 'go', but when I said 'stop' only this one stopped.

C: This one stopped before this one (points to doll further back).

Stage II: six to eight years

The child can recognize that the dolls stopped at the same time, but is uncertain whether the dolls moved for the same length of time. Notion of time is based on either the action carried out or the speed at which the action is carried out. The period of time cannot be separated from the distance covered.

Stage II Sample Responses

C: They started together and then they stopped together.
E: Did they both hop for the same length of time?

C: No, this one walked longer because it went further.

Stage III: nine years up

The child can simultaneously consider time in relationship to distance covered and the speed at which it was done.

Stage III Sample Responses

C: They both hopped for the same time. I said 'go,' and then I said 'stop.'

E: How come this one is ahead?

C: He just took longer hops, but they both hopped just as long.

MOVEMENT AND SPEED

In 1928, Einstein asked Piaget if children's first ideas of speed included an understanding of it as a function of time and distance, or if their first notions of it were more intuitive and primitive.

Paralleling the child's construction of concepts of time are his constructions of concepts of movement and speed.

Developmental Stages

Early in life the child becomes aware of things passing or overtaking. He perceives objects, such as toys, passing him and changing their position in space. On the basis of such experiences, he gradually learns that certain events follow each other in order. It is these notions of order that underlie the development of ideas about movement and speed.

The child of four or five years has an idea of direct order, but cannot yet reverse the order. For example, he can predict the order in which three objects will emerge from a tunnel, but becomes confused when asked to predict in what order they will emerge from the tunnel on the return trip. In the course of play and experimentation, he gradually acquires such concepts as successive order, reverse order, changes of position and their effect on order, changes in direction, and relative movements.

The young child cannot coordinate both starting point and stopping point. He focuses on one aspect of a situation, and believes that two cars cover the same distance if they end up at the same place. He believes that one car travels further if it ends up ahead of another, regardless of the distance covered. Gradually he learns to consider that he has to take into account both starting and stopping points, in regard to speed. He is then able to conclude that, if two cars start and stop at the same time, and one has covered a greater distance, it must have traveled faster. Thus, he constantly readjusts and corrects earlier intuitive notions until he can take into account not only the order of passing, but the distance and time as well. At about the age of eleven, he is able to form a concept of speed as the relationship between distance and time.

* * *

Question: **Does the child** *judge speed?* **Can the child relate distance and time?**

Materials: 2 toy cars of different colors

Instructions:

Ask the child to watch the two cars have a race. Start one car at a point behind the other, but start both cars at the same time. Move one up gradually so that it catches up to the other. Stop both at the same time and at the same point.

E: Which car went faster?
   Did they start together, at the same time?
   Did they stop together, at the same time?
   Did they both go for the same amount of time?

Analysis

Stage I: under five years

Child judges by finishing point alone and believes the cars travel at the same speed. Conceives of speed in relation only to positions, not to time or distance traveled.

Stage I Sample Responses

Child 1

C: Both went at the same speed.
E: How do you know?
C: Because one went as fast as the other.
E: Did one go a longer distance?
C: Yes, the blue one.
E: Then was one going faster than the other?
C: No.

Child 2

C: The blue one went faster.
E: How do you know?
C: Because it was first.
E: Did they stop at the same place.
C: Yes.
E: So they went at the same speed?
C: Yes.

Stage II: six to eight years

Intermediate reactions; the child gradually corrects himself. He equates catching up with speed.

Stage II Sample Responses

Child 1

E: Did they start together?
C: Yes.
E: Did they stop together?
C: Yes.
E: Which one was faster?
C: Red was faster.
E: Did they go the same distance?
C: No, blue is longer.

Child 2

E: Did they start together?
C: No.

E: Which one was in front?

C: No, both started the same.

E: Which one went faster?

C: Red was faster and it finished at the same time as blue.

E: How do you know?

C: Because I saw that blue went further ahead than red. So, red went faster because it came up to blue.

Stage III: nine years

Can take into account both stopping and starting positions. Relations of speed now expressed in terms of distance.

Stage III Sample Responses

E: Did they go at the same speed?

C: No, blue went faster because it had a longer road to do in the same time.

* * *

Question: How does the child *judge distance covered?*

Materials: 2 strings stretched around tacks hammered into 2 boards

2 toy cars

ruler or other measuring instrument

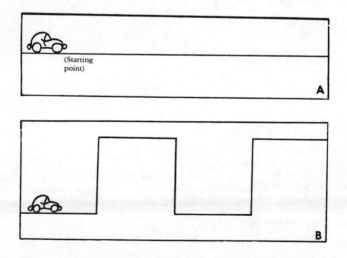

Instructions:

Part 1: Explain to child that each of you will have a car and a road on which it will travel. Child has Board A; Experimenter has Board B. Move your car several segments on B and then ask child to make just as long a trip.

Part 2: Return to starting point. Move your car one segment straight up so that it is at a position equal to the starting point on Board A. Ask child to take a trip just as long. The child either will not move or discover that going the same distance does not necessarily mean arriving at a point corresponding to that on the experimenter's board.

Analysis

Stage I: under six years

Child judges only by the finishing point and believes that two movements are the same length if they arrive at the same finishing point.

Stage I Sample Responses

(The child places car exactly opposite experimenter.)

E: Is that the same distance?

C: Yes.

E: (Experimenter moves two segments.) *Now I'm going this far. You go the same distance.* (The child moves directly opposite)

E: Now I'm going only up to there. You go the same distance. (Moves one segment up directly opposite child's starting point)

C: I can't go forward.

E: Why?

C: Your car is there (point and places car directly opposite experimenter's car.)

E: Do you think that's the same distance?

C: Yes.

E: Why?

C: Because the cars are like that.

E: What does "go the same distance" mean?

C: Coming to the same place.

Stage II: seven to eight years

Child is able to separate distance from points of arrival but cannot measure; usually compares distances visually. Some children begin to use measure, but inaccurately, usually preferring visual check.

Stage II Sample Responses

E: (E travels 2 units. C moves directly opposite.) *Are you sure it's the same distance?*

C: *Yes. No* (starts again). *There* (incorrect).

E: *How can you tell?*

C: *Because I look at the sizes* (checks with fingers).

Stage III: nine years

Child uses measure; realizes a unit of measurement is the best gauge of actual distance covered.

Stage III Sample Responses

Measures by counting the segments and transferring the measuring unit an equal number of times.

* * *

Question: Does the child understand the *order of moving objects in space*? Does the child perceive them as a sequence? Does the child alter his concept of order with changes in the direction of the moving objects?

Materials: 3 large beads: A/black, B/yellow, and C/red (or 3 other colors) threaded on wire or string
3 correspondingly colored crayons for the child to use in responses

Instructions:

Place strung beads in half-closed hand with two ends of wire or thread projecting. Utilize the hand as if it were a tunnel, and make the beads travel from one side to another. The child sees the beads come out in ABC order. Next make the beads retrace their path so that the child sees the beads come out in inverse order, CBA.

E: *In what order will the beads come out at the other side of my hand? What color will come first? What color will come next? Then what color will be next?*

E: *In what order will the beads come out when they go in the opposite direction? What color will come first? What color will be next? What color will be next?*

If the first two questions are answered correctly, rotate the beads, still in ABC order, one half-turn, or 180 degrees, in full view of the child.

E: In what order will the beads come out now? (CBA) *What color will come first? What color will be next? What color will be next?*

The above task can be expanded in number of items and in number of rotations for older children.

Analysis

Stage I: under six years

The child can answer Question #1, not #2. He can predict direct order, not reverse order. The child has no concept of the invariability of the B, or middle, position. He often thinks that of three elements, ABC, in a straight line, B can take precedence, can emerge first, if the direction is changed. He has no concept of "between" as constant.

Stage I Sample Responses

Gets direct order right. When order was reversed, child expected direct order again. Could not predict when rotated. Did not know middle position was invariable.

C: Yellow should have a turn.

Stage II: seven to eight years

Child can reverse order on return journey; he begins to comprehend the invariability of the middle item. Sometimes the child expects direct order to persist in spite of rotation; at other times predicts the right order. He sometimes knows he's wrong, but not why.

Stage III: eight years and up

Correct solution to all problems, even carried to a larger number of items and rotations.

* * *

Question: Does the child understand *concepts of cyclical order?* Does he have a sense of the order of succession of positions in space?

Materials: 4-sided box, or container, each side painted in different
color, or constructed with 4 different colors
8 strips of paper (2 of each color) corresponding with
the colored sides of the box

Instructions:

Show the child each side of the box; name the colors and turn
the box with the child. Then show one color at a time and have
the child show the corresponding paper, thus constructing the
model ABCD (Color A, Color B, Color C, Color D).

Part I: Show the first side, Color A.

E: What color do you think we'll see next as we turn the box?

Child responds by lining up colored strips.

E: What color do you think we'll see next after (name the last
color) *as we turn the box?*

Continue with next color. Proceed with two cycles, ABCD ABCD.
Now start the cycle from colors B and C, the intermediate
positions, and repeat the questions.

Part II: Now demonstrate that the box can be turned in either
direction. Have the child match each side as the box is turned by
choosing the matching colored strip of paper and constructing the
model DCBA. Show first color, Color D.

*E: What color do you think we'll see next as we turn the box this
way?*

Continue with next color.

*E: What color do you think we'll see next as we turn the box this
way?*

Continue with next color. Proceed with two cycles, DCBA DCBA.

Analysis

Stage I: up to five years

The child does not understand the order of succession in a
series. Some of the younger children cannot translate the order
into a sequence to construct a model.

Stage I Sample Responses

1. As the box is rotated, the child places ABC correctly, then

puts D in front of A. When A reappears he puts it under the
first A.

2. Arrives at ABCCDA, then removes one C, but places the
successive colors in order BABCDAA.

Stage II: six to seven years

At first order is understood, but not if started from an
intermediate position, B or C, and inverse order DCBA is not
understood. Gradually the child learns to understand order, both
regular and inverse, even when starting from intermediate positions, but has difficulty picking up continuation of the cycle.

Stage II Sample Responses

C: (Constructs the model ABCD.)

E: What comes next?

C: ABCD.

E: And after this?

C: (Box at C.)

E: What would come next?

C: CBAD.

E: And after this?

C: (Box at B.) *CBDB.* (Child could not do inverse series.)

Successful with cycle ABCDABCD, but when asked to begin with
C, the child constructs CBDA, then CDBA. When starting with B,
BCAD.

Stage III: seven to eight years

Concept is operational. Order is understood, even if started
from an intermediate position, both regular and inverse. Continuation of the cycle, both regular and inverse, is understood.

Stage III Sample Responses

C: (Constructs ABCD.) *Is that difficult?*

E: And if we begin at C?

C: It depends on the way you're going.

E: Like the last time.

C: Oh then it's CDABCD.

E: And if I turn it this way? What comes after C then?

C: BADCBA.

Chapter 3

PROFILE CHARTS

Chart I

INDIVIDUAL PROFILE CHART:

Child's Name:			

Age:		Date:	

Experimenter:

Place an x in appropriate column.
    x's may be connected to construct profile.

TASK:	Stage I	Stage II	Stage III
Conservation – number, equal			
Conservation – number, unequal			
Conservation – liquid			
Conservation – distance			
Conservation area – abstract			
Conservation area – representational			
Conservation – weight			
Conservation – volume			
Classification – spontaneous, geometric			
Classification – spontaneous, representational			
Class inclusion – geometric			
Class inclusion – representational			
Multiple			
Seriation – simple			
Seriation – multiple			
Concept of dreams			
Concept of life			
Floating/sinking			
Causal conjunctions			
Brother/sister			
Right/left			
Reproduction of figures			
Spontaneous measurement			
Construction straight line			
Change of position			
Concept of age			
Age vs. size			
Time/distance			
Judgment of speed			
Judgment of distance			
Cyclical order			
Order vs. direction			
Total:			

Chart II

GROUP PROFILE CHART

Experimenter: Date:

Indicate stage of concept acquisition, 1, 2, or 3, under each child's name, according to task in left hand column

TASK:	Name: Age:																																			
	Name of Child																																			
Conservation – number, equal																																				
Conservation – number, unequal																																				
Conservation – liquid																																				
Conservation – distance																																				
Conservation area – abstract																																				
Conservation area – representational																																				
Conservation – weight																																				
Conservation – volume																																				
Classification – spontaneous, geometric																																				
Classification – spontaneous, representational																																				
Class inclusion – geometric																																				
Class inclusion – representational																																				
Multiple																																				
Seriation – simple																																				
Seriation – multiple																																				
Concept of dreams																																				
Concept of life																																				
Floating/sinking																																				
Causal conjunctions																																				
Brother/sister																																				
Right/left																																				
Reproduction of figures																																				
Spontaneous measurement																																				
Construction straight line																																				
Change of position																																				
Concept of age																																				
Age vs. size																																				
Time/distance																																				
Judgment of speed																																				
Judgment of distance																																				
Cyclical order																																				
Order vs. direction																																				

Chapter 4

ADDITIONAL SOURCES

FURTHER READING

1. Almy, M., Chittenden, C., & Miller, P. *Young Children's Thinking: Studies of Some Aspects of Piaget's Theory.* New York: Teachers College Press, 1966.
2. Athey, J. J. *Educational Implications of Piaget's Theory.* Waltham, Mass.: Ginn, Blaisdell, 1970.
3. Baldwin, A. *Theories of Child Development.* New York: John Wiley, 1967.
4. Beard, R. M. *An Outline of Piaget's Developmental Psychology for Students and Teachers.* New York: Basic Books, 1969.
5. Brearley, M. & Hitchfield, E. *A Guide to Reading Piaget.* New York: Schocken Books, Inc., 1967.
6. Bruner, J. *The Process of Education.* New York: Vintage Books, 1960.
7. Elkind, D. & Flavell, J. (Eds.) *Studies in Cognitive Development: Essays in Honor of Piaget.* New York: Oxford University Press, 1968.
8. Flavell, J. *The Developmental Psychology of Jean Piaget.* Princeton, N. J.: Van Nostrand Co., 1963.
9. Furth, H. *Piaget for Teachers.* Englewood Cliffs, N. J.: Prentice Hall, 1970.
10. Furth, H. & Wachs, H. *Thinking Goes to School.* New York: Oxford University Press, 1974.
11. Ginsburg, H. & Opper, S. *Piaget's Theory of Intellectual Development.* Englewood Cliffs, N. J.: Prentice Hall, Inc., 1969.
12. Hunt, J. McV. *Intelligence and Experience.* New York: Ronald, 1961.
13. Inhelder, B. & Piaget, J. *The Early Growth of Logic in the Child,* New York: Norton, 1969.

14. Inhelder, B. & Piaget, J. *The Growth of Logical Thinking from Childhood to Adolescence.* New York: Basic Books, 1958.
15. Laurendeau, M. & Pinard, A. *Causal Thinking in the Child.* New York: International Universities Press, 1962.
16. Laurendeau, M. & Pinard, A. *The Development of Space in the Child.* New York: International Universities Press, 1970.
17. Lavatelli, C. S. *Piaget's Theory Applied to an Early Childhood Curriculum.* Boston, Mass.: Center for Media Development. American Science and Engineering, Inc., 1970.
18. Lovell, K. *The Growth of Basic Mathematical and Scientific Concepts in Children.* London: University of London Press, Ltd., 1964.
19. Peel, E. A. *The Pupil's Thinking.* London: Oldbourne Press, 1960.
20. Phillips, J. *The Origins of Intellect: Piaget's Theory.* San Francisco: W. H. Freeman and Co., 1969.
21. Piaget, J. *The Child's Conception of Movement and Speed.* New York: Basic Books, 1970.
22. Piaget, J. *The Child's Conception of Number.* New York: Norton, 1965.
23. Piaget, J. *The Child's Conception of Physical Causality.* Totowa, N. J.: Littlefield, Adams & Co., 1960.
24. Piaget, J. *The Child's Conception of the World.* Totowa, N. J.: Littlefield, Adams & Co., 1965.
25. Piaget, J. *The Child's Conception of Time.* New York: Basic Books, 1970.
26. Piaget, J. *The Construction of Reality in the Child.* New York: Basic Books, 1954.
27. Piaget, J. *Judgment and Reasoning in the Child.* Totowa, N. J. Littlefield, Adams & Co., 1959.
28. Piaget, J. *The Language and Thought of the Child.* Cleveland, O.: World Publishing Co., 1955.
29. Piaget, J. *The Origins of Intelligence in Children.* New York; Norton, 1963.
30. Piaget, J. *Play, Dreams, and Imitation in Childhood.* New York: Norton, 1962.
31. Piaget, J. *The Psychology of Intelligence.* New York: Harcourt, Brace, 1950.

32. Piaget, J. *Science of Education and the Psychology of the Child.* New York: Orion Press, 1970.
33. Piaget, J. *Six Psychological Studies.* New York: Random House, 1967.
34. Piaget, J. & Inhelder, B. *The Child's Conception of Space.* New York: Norton, 1967.
35. Piaget, J. & Inhelder, B. *The Psychology of the Child.* New York: Basic Books, 1969.
36. Piaget, J., Inhelder, B. & Szeminska, A. *The Child's Conception of Geometry.* New York: Basic Books, 1960.
37. Pulaski, M. *Understanding Piaget.* New York: Harper and Row, 1971.
38. Richmond, P. *An Introduction to Piaget.* New York: Basic Books, 1971.
39. Ripple, R. & Rockcastle, V. (Eds.) *Piaget Rediscovered.* Ithaca, New York: Cornell University Press, 1964.
40. Schwebel, M. & Raph, J. (Eds.) *Piaget in the Classroom.* New York: Basic Books, 1973.
41. Sigel, I. & Hooper, F. (Eds.) *Logical Thinking in Children: Research Based on Piaget's Theory.* New York: Holt, Rinehart, and Winston, 1968.
42. Sime, M. *A Child's Eye View of Piaget for Parents and Teachers.* London: Thames and Hudson, 1973.
43. Wadsworth, B. *Piaget's Theory of Cognitive Development.* New York: McKay, 1971.

*Numbers 11, 18, 19, 37, and 40 are especially good as introductions.

FILM RESOURCES

AECOM (Albert Einstein College of Medicine) SCALES OF SENSORY MOTOR DEVELOPMENT SERIES – Sibylle Escalona

Causality – 23 minutes, black and white
Object Permanence – 23 minutes, black and white
Spatial Relationships – 40 minutes, black and white
(Available from New York University Film LIbrary)

COGNITION — 30 minutes, color

  (Harper and Row; available from New York University Film Library)

GROWTH AND INTELLIGENCE: An Observational Study of One Child —Formanek, Greenberg, Gurian
 I. Marc at Six Months — 12 minutes, color
 II. Marc at Eighteen Months — 12 minutes, color
III. Marc at Three Years — 20 minutes, color
IV. Marc at Four and a Half — 25 minutes, color

  (I and II available from Center for Media Development, Great Neck, New York; III and IV available from Curriculum Consultants, 13 Oak Brook Lane, Merrick, New York, N. Y

INFANCY — Jerome Kagan, — 20 minutes, color

  (Available from New York University Film Library)

ORDINAL SCALES OF INFANT PSYCHOLOGICAL DEVELOP-MENT — Ina C. Uzgiris and J. McV. Hunt

  Object Permanence — 40 minutes, black and white
  Development of Means — 34 minutes, black and white
  Imitation: Gestural and Vocal — 35 minutes, black and white
  Operational Causality — 21 minutes, black and white
  Object Relations in Space — 28 minutes, black and white
  Development of Schemas — 36 minutes, black and white

  (Available from University of Illinois Visual Aids Service, Champaign, Illinois)

PIAGET'S DEVELOPMENTAL THEORY:

  Classification — 17 minutes, color
  Conservation — 28 minutes, color
  Formal Thought — 32 minutes, color
  Growth of Intelligence in the Pre-School Years — 30 minutes, color

  (Davidson Films: available from New York University Film Library)